Mountain and High Desert
Hideaways

Mountain and High Desert Hideaways

Gladys Montgomery

First published in the United States of America in 2005
by Universe Publishing
A Division of Rizzoli International Publications, Inc.
300 Park Avenue South
New York, NY 10010
www.rizzoliusa.com

Cover photographs:
Front: courtesy of Canadian Rocky
Mountain Resorts
Back: courtesy of Wyndham Hotels

2005 2006 2007 2008 /
10 9 8 7 6 5 4 3 2 1

Graphic Design: Adam Michaels

Printed in China

ISBN: 0-8478-2715-1

Library of Congress Catalog Control Number: 2005900492

Introduction

Go West, young man!
—Horace Greeley

The inherent irony of doing a book about hideaway destinations is that people who have a favorite haunt fear its "discovery" will mean the loss of its true and original character. Many of the places in this book have been around a long time. Although they adapt to new demands, their essence remains unchanged. Many are small by choice. Others, though larger, are unrepentantly individualistic. As long as they are, they will remain hideaways.

In the mountain and desert regions of the West there are two great building traditions: the adobe structures of the deserts, and the log and stone construction of the mountains. Maybe because its landscapes make strong demands, the buildings of the West show a profound pride of place. From generation to generation, new buildings reference old ones. Sun Mountain Lodge, built in the 1990s, recalls Timberline, built in the 1930s. La Posada, built in the 1920s, takes its inspiration from an imagined 1869 Spanish hacienda. Sanctuary on Camelback Mountain stands upon the shoulders of the Modernist who designed the 1950s Orbit In hotel. Some—like a traditional Navajo hogan and a cave seventy feet underground—are unusual and worth seeking out. Others offer civility and respite from the crowds in high traffic destinations like the Grand Canyon and Vail, Colorado, the country's largest ski area. One consists of tents in the high desert under the wide, star-strewn Wyoming sky. Those tents recall one of the West's earliest "building" traditions and an essential message: Out here, nature is the greatest architect.

The destinations featured here offer horseback riding, skiing, fly-fishing, easy access to wilderness areas for hiking or biking, swimming, and a rich array of other activities. Beyond good food, creature comforts, a bit of pampering, and the unparalleled pleasures of the great outdoors, what the places in this book all have in common is a respect for the environment. The unsung heroes behind many of them are environmentalists and historic preservationists, federal and state agencies, and nonprofit institutions that help to ensure the integrity and survival of endangered landscapes, wildlife, and buildings.

At the heart of this book is the notion that buildings are an entry point to a deeper experience of travel. How they came about, who built them and why, why they are where they are, what they're made of and why, how they've been used, why they're furnished as they are— these questions add up to a fascinating social history. They can lead to an understanding that the tourist always misses and the traveler always seeks. Each of the destinations in this book, whether it's a hundred years old, a decade old, or still under construction, has a story as unique as its personality.

You may discover your own special hideaway in this book or you may not. There are a lot more out there. One is waiting for you. Go find it.

GLADYS MONTGOMERY

The Ahwahnee

Yosemite Park is…a refuge…in which one gains the advantages of both solitude and society…. This one noble park is big enough and rich enough for a whole life of study and aesthetic enjoyment…. Its natural beauty cleans and warms like a fire, and you will be willing to stay forever in one place like a tree.
—John Muir, 1911

NOBLE BUILDING, NOBLE SETTING, NOBLE CAUSE

John Muir, one of America's great environmentalists, began exploring the Sierra Nevada in 1869. In 1890, just as the U.S. Congress was about to vote on the creation of the country's third national park at Yosemite, he published an article describing Yosemite's wonders—the High Sierra, which he called the Range of Light, Tuolumne Meadows, the Great Tuolumne Canyon, the Lyell Glacier, Lake Tenaya, and its geysers, more in one location than anywhere else in the world. Muir, who founded the Sierra Club, was influential in the creation of Yosemite National Park, but he was not the first to be struck by Yosemite's grandeur.

The Yosemite Valley was historically the home of the Miwok Indians, whose ancestors had inhabited it for more than 4,000 years. The Miwok lived in the Sierra Nevada's western foothills, following deer herds to the high country each spring and summer and returning in the fall to villages along the Merced River. Ahwahnee, or "gaping mouth," was their name for the valley. In 1849, when gold was discovered in the Sierra Nevada, thousands of miners moved into the area,   followed by cattle ranchers who called the Indians "Yosemites," a corruption of the native word for grizzly bear. When the Miwoks refused to sign a treaty giving up their land, a battalion was organized to remove them. In 1851, the battalion followed them into Yosemite Valley, and its members were awestruck.

One wrote, "As I looked, a peculiar exalted sensation seemed to fill my whole being, and I found my eyes in tears with emotion." The Miwok remained in their ancestral home, but word of the valley's beauty soon spread. Visitors came by stagecoach and horseback, entrepreneurs built hotels and houses, ranchers grazed livestock in subalpine meadows, and settlers planted orchards. These encroachments damaged Yosemite's ecosystem.

One early visitor was Carleton Watkins, a self-taught San Francisco photographer who first visited the valley and the Mariposa Grove in 1861. To capture the West's vast landscapes, Watkins used a large, heavy camera to make mammoth eighteen-by-twenty-two-inch negatives, which he transported, with a tripod, glass plates, and a portable darkroom over precarious trails to "the best spot with the best view." He also used a stereo camera to produce two near-identical images of the same scene, which created an illusion of three dimensions when viewed through a stereoscope, a popular entertainment in Victorian parlors. Watkins' sophisticated images transformed fabled wilderness into visual reality for an incredulous public. After seeing the first important photographic records of Yosemite, New York landscape artist Albert Bierstadt was impelled to make his initial trip. In that and subsequent visits, Bierstadt created some of his most magnificent landscapes—Yosemite Falls, Bridal Veil Falls, Half Dome, Hetch Hetchy Canyon and Valley, and Merced River. California senator John Conness, who owned a set of Watkins' prints, drafted the 1864 law that President Abraham Lincoln signed, granting Yosemite Valley and the Mariposa Grove of Giant Sequoias to the state of California, marking the first time in history that the federal government established a public trust to protect scenic lands and preserve them for public benefit.

Despite its protected status, Yosemite still faced threats. At the turn of the century, the city of San Francisco lobbied to dam the Tuolumne River. Muir led efforts opposing the plan, but lost in 1913. By 1901, automobiles were already entering the park; by 1907, the Yosemite Valley Railroad was completed,

The Ahwahnee
Yosemite National Park
California
559-252-4848
www.yosemitepark.com

Opposite: The Ahwahnee, in the Yosemite Valley, is one of the most impressive and upscale lodgings in America's national park system. Its site, rugged materials, and massing make this landmark a treasured part of Yosemite's landscape. The majestic Yosemite Falls.

bringing more visitors. Increased tourism meant increased demand for facilities and more need for sensible environmental management.

This was true in all the national parks, so in 1916, Congress created the National Park Service. Its first director was Stephen Mather, and Yosemite was his favorite park. In 1925, Mather ordered construction of a first-class, year-round hotel to attract elite visitors. Harvard-trained Los Angeles architect Gilbert Stanley Underwood, who served as the consulting architect for the Union Pacific Railroad and had completed the lodges at Zion and Bryce Canyon Parks, was commissioned to design it. He chose a site in Yosemite Valley, the centerpiece of the park. The hotel was placed against the backdrop of the Royal Arches, with views of Yosemite Falls, Glacier Point, and Half Dome.

Underwood designed the Ahwahnee, which would become known as the greatest achievement of his long and successful association with the National Park Service, with three wings extending from a central tower six stories high. The north wing consists of an entry lobby and two floors of private rooms; the south wing has the Great Lounge, meeting rooms, and three floors of private rooms; and the west wing is devoted to an enormous dining room. The design is asymmetrical with jutting chimneys, decks, and porches that echo the jagged lines of the Royal Arches behind it. Because of fear of fire, the primary building materials were steel, granite, stone, and concrete. The beams and siding were cast in molds scored to look like timber, then stained to imitate redwood.

The building contractor promised to complete the project in less than four months "for a maximum guaranteed cost of $525,000, including our fee...." In what

one newspaper hailed as "one of the most remarkable accomplishments in California automotive history," truckers worked seven days a week, hauling 1,000 tons of structural steel, 5,000 tons of building stone, 30,000 board feet of timber, $25,000 worth of kitchen equipment, and 60 percent of the furnishings over primitive roads to the site. None of the materials was taken from within the park. Some 18,000 square feet were added to the plan, and the project ultimately cost more than $1.25 million and took eleven months to complete. What its creators accomplished can be fully appreciated when standing in the Great Lounge with its soaring twenty-four-foot beamed ceiling, stained-glass windows, and massive cut-sandstone fireplaces, or in the spectacular 6,630-square-foot dining room where the beamed, vaulted ceiling rises to thirty-four feet, and floor-to-ceiling windows offer a view that is beyond compare.

The Ahwahnee's original decoration was by art historians Phyllis Ackerman and Arthur Pope, a husband-and-wife team who based their designs on the baskets of California's Indian tribes. For the Great Lounge, they chose the massive English oak tables, secretaries, and Gothic wrought-iron chandeliers that still furnish it. A museum-quality collection of original rugs decorates the walls, and Native American designs crown each guest-room door. Jeannette Dyer Spencer, a San Francisco artist who became the hotel's resident designer, created the stained-glass panels that top the windows in the Great Lounge and the mural above the fireplace in the elevator lobby. Although the Ahwahnee's lounge and dining room are enormous, many of its public rooms, like the Solarium and the Mural Room, with its Arts and Crafts–style depiction of Yosemite's flora and fauna, are more intimate and equally grand. The 150,000-square-foot main building contains ninety-nine guest rooms, including seven suites. Eight bungalows in the woods near the Merced River offer an additional twenty-four rooms.

During World War II, the hotel was a rest-and-relaxation hospital for Navy personnel. The Great Lounge, used as a dormitory, accommodated 350 men. Between 1943 and 1946, 90,000 servicemen and

Opposite: The hotel's soaring lines echo the rocky Royal Arches behind it. Once through the entryway, park visitors can also choose tent accommodations. This page: Yosemite's Half Dome and Valley still astonish visitors.

servicewomen relaxed in the park, and 6,752 patients were treated at the Ahwahnee.

During the seasons, there's skiing, snowboarding, ice skating, snowshoeing, hiking, biking, fishing, swimming, rafting, horseback riding, and rock climbing in one of the world's premier rock-climbing areas, with expert instruction at the Yosemite Mountaineering School. There's also golf nearby at the Wawona Hotel, on a circa 1918 course. In this setting golfers may feel that life's most important scores aren't measured in par. Yosemite's landscape inspires larger thoughts, like the democratic notion that it be preserved for everyone to enjoy.

Ever since Watkins first photographed it, Yosemite has been a photographer's paradise, one place where everyone should take a camera. Ansel Adams, one of America's best-known photographers, took his first snapshots of Yosemite Valley in 1916, at the age of fourteen, with a Brownie box camera. "I knew my destiny," he said, "when I first experienced Yosemite." As Muir had said, Yosemite provided a lifetime of inspiration and material: Adams returned there nearly every year for the rest of his life. In a career that spanned more than sixty years, Adams created some 40,000 negatives and developed thousands of prints. He became a director of the Sierra Club and supporter of the Wilderness Society and an environmental advocate. When he died at the age of eighty-four, Congress named a wilderness area south of the park in his honor, and the U.S. Geological Survey designated an 11,760-foot peak "Mount Ansel Adams." Adams called the peaks of the Sierra Nevada "high altars." His images of Yosemite's grandeur are visual hymns celebrating the presence of God in nature.

Though the young Adams played a court jester in the Ahwahnee's fabled multinight Bracebridge Dinner at Christmastime, he professed not to like the building, which he said "tried to compete with the environment" and lost. Now that the structure has weathered and settled into its surroundings, guests may disagree with him. Like the natural features Adams photographed, the Ahwahnee seems an integral part of Yosemite's legacy.

This page: The Great Lounge features Native American motifs, stained-glass windows, and a 24-foot beamed ceiling. Opposite: Architectural details add to the magnificence of the 6,630-square-foot dining room and make the commodious guest rooms interesting.

Amangani

There is a muscular energy in sunlight corresponding to the spirtual energy of the wind.
—Annie Dillard

BOLDNESS AND BRAVADO
IN THE GRAND TETONS

Amangani is a bold building. It almost has a feeling of prehistory—rough sandstone ramparts at its base, wood above, hewing to the crest of East Gros Ventre Butte 7,000 feet above sea level. The strong lines of its central core assert themselves against the mountainscape while its flanking wooden structures reach into it, creating a building that appears both ageless and, against this ancient backdrop, oddly impermanent. The three-story resort follows the earth's contours, its hipped roof of sod and cedar takes its form from natural outcroppings. Inside, Amangani is a counterbalance of textures— smooth, polished Pacific redwood and cedar, floor-to-ceiling columns of rough Oklahoma sandstone—with vistas inward through sweeping spaces and outward to the Snake River Range and Spring Gulch.

Located at the southern end of Jackson Hole, just twenty minutes from the Jackson airport and some of the best skiing in the West, Amangani's contemporary design is a synergy of Asian and Native American influences. The name Amangani derives from "aman," the Sanskrit word for "peaceful" and "gani," the Shoshone Indian word for "home." Its decor juxtaposes soft carpeting and stone floors, rough-woven rawhide and rattan chairs with faux-fur cushions, slate with sisal, and severe terrazzo pedestal tables with side tables hewn from the hefty trunks of pines. Each of Amangani's forty modern, spare, and luxurious suites has a deck, a fireplace, a king-size platform bed, and a window-side daybed. Lighting positioned behind cedar planks casts a soft glow and turns function into sculpture. As one would expect in this modern setting, rooms are equipped with data plug-in and high-speed Internet access.

Opposite: Built of rock and timber and roofed with sod, Amangani, whose name derives from the Sanskrit word for "peaceful" and the Shoshone Indian word for "home," follows the contours of the earth, blending into Wyoming's summer landscape.

A long wall of windows spanning the lounge, library, and dining room offers views across the valley to the Teton Pass, which divides the Snake River Range from the Teton Range. Guests have free range of Amangani's library, which houses a collection of fiction, CDs, and books about Western art, Native American culture, the region's flora and fauna, and the two great national parks, Grand Teton and Yellowstone, that are nearby. Amangani's health center is fully equipped and offers personal training and spa and salon services. Its 115-foot heated outdoor pool and its 113-foot-square whirlpool finished in quartzite tile overlook the snowcapped Tetons, and, at sunset, are extraordinary places from which to enjoy the view.

In the dining room, people tuck into regionally produced organic foods, hefty steaks, chops, and seafood beneath sculpted metal panels, with images of elk rendered in a style that recalls ancient American Indian pictographs. It's an apt image: The National Elk Refuge is just a short distance away.

At the southern end of the greater Yellowstone area, the resort's site is a vast expanse of meadows and mountains, sage flats, wildlife refuges, national forests, and Grand Teton and Yellowstone National Parks. The 25,000-acre National Elk Refuge, created in 1912, the only refuge in the U.S. Fish and Wildlife Service devoted primarily to elk, provides a winter home with substantial forage for as many as 10,000 elk that spend the summer in Grand Teton National Park, Bridger-Teton National Forest, or in the southern part of Yellowstone National Park. In 1995, American gray wolves were reintroduced to Yellowstone, and in 1999, they returned to the refuge for the first time in sixty years.

At the Elk Refuge is the National Museum of Wildlife Art, a ruggedly designed sandstone building that houses 2,500 works from the early nineteenth century to the present. Jackson Hole Museum traces the growth of the area from the time Lewis and Clark first traversed it, to the time when trappers and mountain men such as Jim Bridger found the area a rich source of beaver and other valuable furs. Jackson Hole is rich not just in natural life but in art, with more than twenty-five galleries of paintings, pottery, jewelry, photographs, sculpture, and crafts.

Amangani
1535 North East Butte Road
Jackson, WY 83001
877-734-7333
www.amanresorts.com

About a half day's drive away, northwest of Lander, Wyoming, is the 1.7-million-acre Wind River Reservation, established in 1864. Home to the Northern Arapaho and Eastern Shoshone tribes, it contains two museums devoted to their cultures; the grave of Sacajawea, the Shoshone woman who guided Lewis and Clark; and Fort Washakie, the only American military fort named for an Indian chief. (Washakie advised General George Armstrong Custer not to attack at Little Big Horn.) In the summer, powwows with traditional Indian dancing, music, and food are held frequently. Beyond the reservation, in Cody, Wyoming, the Buffalo Bill Historical Center comprises five museums showcasing some of the finest Western art in the world and a museum of natural history. Because of its superlative collection, the center has been called "the Smithsonian of the West." Among the artists whose works the museum exhibits are Frederick Remington, whose images of Native Americans and cowboys helped to create the popular myth of the West; Charles M. Russell, whose approximately 4,000 artworks include many realistic studies depicting Native American women; Edgar Samuel Paxson, whose frontier life informed his work as a painter and is best known for Custer's Last Stand; Earl Biss, a member of the Absaroka Crow tribe, whose abstract paintings capture the forces of nature; and William Henry Jackson, who accompanied explorer Ferdinand Hayden's 1870s expeditions and took the first important photographs of Yellowstone.

The town of Jackson is a convenient gateway to Grand Teton National Park and Yellowstone National Park. Amangani is perfectly situated to take full

Opposite: Amangani's bold exterior matches the grandeur of the Tetons, while fine detailing brings intimacy to generously proportioned interior spaces. This page: The lounge's floor-to-ceiling windows and simple contemporary furnishings ensure that the focus is on the view.

advantage of all the area has to offer, but at enough of a remove to feel secluded.

In winter, Jackson averages 400 inches of snow. The two mountains that make up the Jackson Hole Mountain Resort boast plenty of Alpine excitement and one of the greatest lift-served vertical drops in North America. Amangani runs a shuttle to and from the resort and maintains a ski lounge just under one hundred feet from the lifts. There's Nordic skiing nearby at the Spring Creek Nordic Center, snowmobiling, snowshoeing, sleigh rides, and dogsledding with teams training for Alaska's grueling Iditarod race.

In the warm months, the area is a naturalist's paradise, a seasonal home to pronghorn antelope, bison, moose, Great Gray owls, and lettuce-green and trumpeter swans. Guests can hike, mountain climb in the Tetons, mountain bike, or horseback ride at Spring Creek Stables, within walking distance of Amangani. The Snake River has terrific white-water rafting, and its South Fork is reputed to be one of the West's premier places for fly-fishing, though anglers will find plenty to satisfy in the area's countless rivers, streams, and lakes. Many of the resort's guests choose to tour the area, including Yellowstone, with a private Amangani excursion guided by a naturalist; explore Grand Teton National Park's more than 200 miles of trails; observe the estimated 300 bird species that inhabit the area around Jackson Hole; or get a bird's-eye view from a hot-air balloon. The Jackson Hole rodeo takes place twice a week all summer, and the Grand Teton music festival runs during July and August. Golfers have two eighteen-hole championship courses to choose from in Jackson Hole: Teton Pines, designed by Arnold Palmer, and Jackson Hole Golf and Tennis, designed by Robert Trent Jones; both have tennis courts and offer instruction.

Whatever outdoor activity people choose, the great outdoors is nowhere greater than here. The national parks, national forests, and other protected wilderness areas cut a wide swath across the West, and, taken together, comprise the largest section of public lands in the United States. The twelve million acres of "the Greater Yellowstone Ecosystem" are astonishing for their ecological integrity, and for the species of plant

and animal life that remain relatively undisturbed.

For sheer grandeur, one need only look as far as the Tetons, the youngest mountains in the Rockies, which rise more than 7,000 feet above the valley of Jackson Hole. The forty-mile-long mountain front with eight peaks over 12,000 feet is the focal point of Grand Teton National Park. The Tetons have their footing in hard crystalline bedrock formed more than 2.5 billion years ago, overlaid with sedimentary rock and deposited as layers of sand, mud, and lime by great inland seas some 500 million years ago. These layers are visible in "The Wall," the soaring cliff of stratified rocks seen when looking west from Jackson Hole, and the Gros Ventre Mountains contain vast exposures of colorful sedimentary rocks formed as recently as 100 million years ago. Jackson Hole and other valleys were sculpted by glaciers.

Amangani, with its massive lines, rugged materials tamed for human comfort, and simplicity, pays homage to nature, which, as this landscape reminds us, creates the most stunning architecture of all.

This page: The guest rooms derive their comforting ambience from polished wood, subtle lighting, warming fires, and clean lines. Opposite: At the pool, precise angles, smooth surfaces, and rugged materials create a spectacular setting from which to admire the mountains.

Arcosanti

We of an older generation can get along with what we have, though with growing hardship; but in your full manhood and womanhood you will want what nature once so bountifully supplied and man so thoughtlessly destroyed; and because of that want you will reproach us, not for what we have used, but for what we have wasted....
—Theodore Roosevelt, Message to the Schoolchildren of the United States, 1907

ESCAPE TO A PIONEERING CITY ON A HILL

Although it has been in existence for more than thirty years, Arcosanti is something brand-new. The brainchild of architect Paolo Soleri, it is an urban laboratory where structures and systems represent a marriage of architecture and ecology—a concept Soleri calls 'arcology.' Located outside of Cordes Junction, just seventy miles north of Phoenix, Arcosanti is a far remove in concept from any other city in the United States. Its sweeping curves and shadowed angles, dynamic arches, and soaring walls of concrete dominate a high mesa in the Arizona desert, a dense cluster in the midst of agricultural fields and wilderness. Begun in 1970 and less than 10 percent completed, Arcosanti is a work in progress, with a population of less than one hundred where a planned 7,000 may someday live. With just ten simple guest rooms and one apartment suite for visitors, Arcosanti offers the opportunity not just to escape, but to experience the sort of built environment Soleri believes will be essential if humans are to survive and thrive on this planet.

Sustainability is not a new idea, but in Soleri's view it is an urgent one. The world's population passed the six billion mark in 1999, and, according to United Nations' projections, will increase to 8.9 billion by 2050, with 90 percent of people living in what are now considered the less developed regions of the world—Asia, Africa, and Latin America. Paralleling this development is another:

Opposite: Arcosanti is a work in progress, an experiment designed by visionary architect Paolo Soleri to demonstrate how the city of the future might function. An educational enterprise, it combines ecological building principles with culture, agriculture, and recreation.

A majority of the world's population now lives in cities. Though Europe and North America contain only a small portion of the world's population, they use a huge proportion of its material resources. Population growth, coupled with a global need to increase or reallocate water, fuel, food, and other resources, including space for shelter and human activity, will place tremendous stress on the planet.

Soleri immigrated to the United States from Italy in 1947 and studied with Frank Lloyd Wright. Like Wright, Soleri's focus is on buildings that harmonize with their environments. However, for the past forty years, Soleri has looked beyond form and materials and single-family dwellings of the sort Wright designed to address a different set of problems. His concern is that the American model of urban sprawl and suburban development, with its massive land requirements, sizable structures, orientation toward consumerism, and required infrastructure, is a wasteful use of resources. Soleri's concept of arcology posits compact cities that minimize the use of land, raw materials, and energy, thereby reducing waste and environmental pollution, providing ready access to the surrounding natural environments, and affording privacy—yet maximizing the kind of dynamic interactions that have been the hallmark of history's most successful and culturally significant cities, from the ancient Anasazi's Pueblo Bonito to the Italian cities of the Renaissance. "It is a very old story," Soleri maintains. "There's no separation between the appearance of the cities and the development of civilizations." Arcosanti is the prototype of this concept, a testing ground for ideas that might be used in the future.

Its dense cluster of multiuse buildings, amphitheaters, studios, and shaded plazas contain work space, housing, restaurants, and services, as well as places to gather and enjoy music, poetry readings, plays, dance, and other cultural activities. Living, working, and public spaces are within easy reach of each other, eliminating the need for cars within the city. By design, the land on which Arcosanti's buildings are sited is unsuitable for agriculture. Yet, in the midst of 860 acres with an additional 3,000 leased acres, Arcosanti is surrounded by fields for crops, gardens, and orchards, and incorporates

Arcosanti
HC 74, Box 4136
Mayer, AZ 86333
928-632-7135
www.arcosanti.org

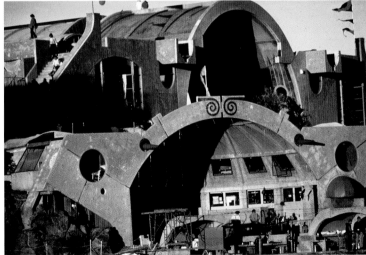

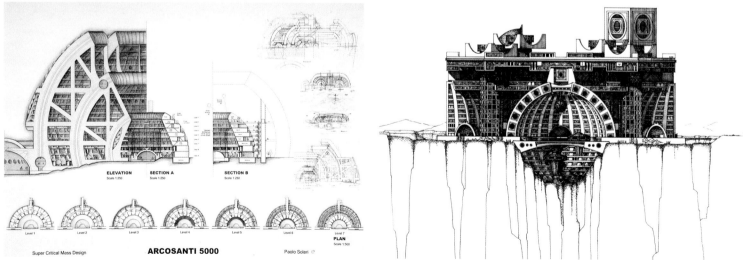

ELEVATION
Scale 1:250

SECTION A
Scale 1:250

SECTION B
Scale 1:250

Level 1　Level 2　Level 3　Level 4　Level 5　Level 6　Level 7

PLAN
Scale 1:500

Super Critical Mass Design

ARCOSANTI 5000

Paolo Soleri

greenhouses and edible landscaping. In its fifteen acres of agricultural fields, vegetable gardens, greenhouses, and orchards, Arcosanti uses no synthetic or chemical herbicides, pesticides, or fertilizers, relying instead on compost and natural soil enhancers. Herbs are grown for culinary and medicinal use; flowers please the senses and attract beneficial insects and birds; many of the plants offer shade and moisture in summer. Microclimates created by the buildings enable the growing of plants that would not normally survive here.

Arcosanti's swimming pool is tucked next to a cliff, overlooking the desert, and the city's proximity to the Agua Fria River and the mountains of the Agua Fria National Monument means that recreational opportunities are just a short distance away.

Constructed of concrete, Arcosanti is not a "green" structure per se, but it employs energy-wise approaches on a large scale. Though it draws most of its energy from the grid, it also produces power from solar panels and a windmill. Its buildings, up to five stories in height, use passive solar techniques that reduce energy use for heating, lighting, and cooling. At an elevation of 3,750 feet, Arcosanti's high mesa site affords cooler temperatures than nearby desert cities. Greenhouses, and the application of greenhouse principles to glass doors and windows, are used to regulate heat. There's an emphasis on cross-ventilation to channel breezes through interiors. Large south-facing windows allow the low winter sun to enter and its warmth to be absorbed by the concrete walls. In summer, when the sun is higher in the sky, less light and heat enter, and windows are equipped with seasonal fabric shades, which Soleri calls "garment architecture." Even large windows are opened in the evening to allow the cooler night air to enter. A café is partially heated by air warmed by a skylight, then blown through a fabric tube into its atrium. Huge, visually dramatic, and highly efficient apses—quarter spheres set on end and open to the south—capture the heat in winter and provide shade in summer. In one such structure, exhaust heat from Arcosanti's foundry furnace, used to produce bronze wind-bells that are sold to support the project, is ducted through adjacent living areas and stored in concrete heat sinks to provide heat in winter.

Opposite: Soleri's early drawings were given substance in Arizona by construction crews of students and volunteers. This page: A concrete- and cast-silt "vault" accommodates concerts and other activities. Sun-heated air, blown through a fabric tube, warms the café.

Small ponds outside buildings provide evaporative cooling to interiors. In the Lab, which contains construction functions, a large glass skylight is whitewashed in summer to provide shade, and air is channeled through the north and south doors, so the building remains comfortably cool. Composting and recycling are part of life here, and biological processes are used to treat sewage and wastewater.

Arcosanti's modern architecture incorporates eye-pleasing forms like curved windows, arches, and open staircases, and the decorative potential of concrete. Interiors are flooded with natural light and appointed with wood details; bathroom floors are done with ceramic tile murals made on site. Prior to designing Arcosanti, Soleri was a ceramist, working with cast silt, a process whereby earthen molds prepared with pigments are used to shape and color concrete forms. Silt-cast concrete forms are used on a massive scale, in the arching enclosures Soleri calls the Vaults, which are used for performances and banquets, and on a more intimate scale in interior ceilings, like the one in Sky Suite, available to guests. This two-bedroom apartment with a living room and kitchen features a roof terrace with growing fruits and vegetables and a 360-degree view of the landscape, one of many terrific views offered by Arcosanti's rooftops.

Structures incorporate concrete and steel beams, poured-in-place concrete, and cast concrete. In the apses, lower sections consist of poured-in-place concrete, while upper curved panels were precast on silt, lifted into place with a crane, and connected with weld plates and beams at the top. Since Arcosanti is a city in the making, there are ample opportunities to watch it take form, with skilled professionals and volunteers from Arcosanti's educational workshops working side by side. Besides its foundry, Arcosanti has fully equipped shops for woodworking, architectural modeling, painting, and welding. To date, more than 5,000 volunteers have participated in its construction.

Since multiuse structures and easy access to cultural activities are key concepts at Arcosanti, guests can enjoy performances at the Colly Soleri Music Center, a 350-seat concert hall named for Soleri's late wife. They

can shop and eat at one of Arcosanti's multifunction buildings called Crafts III, which contains a bakery, a café serving breakfast, lunch, and dinner buffets, residences, a visitor center, and a gallery. It's a great space, with views of the desert, natural lighting, and a huge atrium looking out from the café to the gallery; a shop that sells, among other things, books and documentary videos about Arcosanti; Soleri's sculptures and work by resident artists; and cast-bronze and ceramic windbells, produced on site. These help finance Arcosanti's construction, the nonprofit Cosanti educational foundation, and more than twenty-five other charitable organizations. Arcosanti offers architectural tours, silt sculpture and other workshops, bird-watching tours, foreign language instruction, and organic-garden tours. Because Arcosanti is also an experiential educational institution, guests are welcome to apply for its seminars or five-week workshop programs to learn more about the concept of arcology and to work to build Arcosanti. Soleri's residence and sculpture studio, Cosanti, which also offers tours, is not far away.

"We must realize that we are part of something bigger than ourselves and act in accord with that," Soleri says. "The larger view needn't be sacrificial. It can be a most incredible leap into something really very exciting." Our communities, he says, "should become a more lively container for the social, cultural, and spiritual evolution of [mankind]." One of the country's foremost ecologically sensitive communities, Arcosanti combines architecture, nature, and art in the most modernistic of settings. Here, along with views of spectacular desert sunsets and an escape from the ordinary, guests may find glimpses into the city of the future and ideas to take home.

This page: Arcosanti has ten guest rooms and one suite for visitors. Opposite: A pool atop the mesa overlooks agricultural fields. Orchards and regal cedars surround Arcosanti's greenhouses, which supply produce for the city's residents and guests.

Belton Chalet

It was in Glacier, with its towering peaks, surefooted mountain goats, and romanticized Native Americans, that the Great Northern defined an image of what made the West a region of mythic character and a place where ordinary Americans could experience extraordinary things.

—Larry M. Dilsaver and William Wyckoff,
The Geographical Review, 1997

AN EXTRAORDINARY EXPERIENCE
IN AN EXTRAORDINARY PLACE

Built in 1910 by the Grand Northern Railroad in anticipation of the creation of Glacier National Park, Belton Chalet is a rarity: an intimate, perfectly restored park lodge outside and just west of the park entrance. Guests sit on broad balconies in rocking chairs, wander its heritage gardens, sleep in vintage iron beds, and take off toward Lake McDonald just as visitors did a hundred years ago. Despite its twenty-first-century comforts, including a small spa, Belton Chalet seems to belong to the past.

With about 1.4 million acres of wilderness and some of the most spectacular mountain scenery in America, Glacier was America's tenth national park, set aside by Congress in 1910. Its geological features, varied animal and plant life, and relative remoteness combine to make it one of the largest and most intact ecosystems in North America. The only national park in America linked with one in Canada, Glacier is a monument to the efforts of George Bird Grinnell, who spearheaded its creation.

Grinnell, who studied at Yale and attended a school run by John James Audubon's widow, served as a naturalist on George Armstrong Custer's 1874 expedition to the Black Hills, where he began his study of the Pawnee, Gros Ventre, and Cheyenne tribes. An advocate of Indian rights, Grinnell helped draft several treaties. A champion of environmental protection, he edited and published *Forest and Stream* magazine, founded the

Audubon Society, advocated timber and wildlife management, documented Yellowstone's flora and fauna, and developed the conservation philosophy expressed in Theodore Roosevelt's presidential policies.

In 1898, while climbing Mount Rainier with the head of the U.S. Department of Interior and the chief of the U.S. Forest Service, Grinnell got lost. The party was rescued by photographer Edward S. Curtis. Two years later, Grinnell took Curtis to visit Montana's Blackfeet Indians. "Take a good look," Grinnell told Curtis. "We're not going to see this kind of thing much longer. It already belongs to the past." Curtis had been photographing Native Americans in the Seattle area where he had his studio, but what Grinnell said set him on his life's mission. Curtis embarked on a thirty-year project, traveling 40,000 miles, photographing and interviewing members of almost a hundred tribes, and creating an incomparable record of their cultures. The Blackfeet sold the land that became Glacier National Park to the U.S. government in 1895. Efforts to establish the park began shortly afterward.

Besides Grinnell, the park had two other important champions: railroad tycoon James Jerome Hill, founder of the Great Northern, and his son Louis. The railroad inaugurated service in the area in 1893, and the park sat strategically on its trunk line between Minneapolis and Seattle.

Louis Hill became an honorary member of the Blackfeet tribe, and Great Northern's publicity linked Glacier, more than any other national park, with Native Americans. Blackfeet were employed in the park and even went on nationwide tour to represent it. In 1913, a Blackfeet Indian modeled for the new Buffalo nickel. The Hills did yeoman service in developing Montana, offering reduced fares to immigrants, advertising land availability outside the United States, promoting modern agricultural methods, even giving away livestock to farmers. Fittingly, the Great Northern's premier luxury train was called the Empire Builder. It made a two-night stop at Glacier. There was money to be made in tourism.

The Great Northern coined the slogan "See America First." Promoters of America's national parks, beginning with Yellowstone in 1872, reasoned that wealthy tourists

Belton Chalet
P.O. Box 206
West Glacier, MT 59936
888-BELTON5
www.beltonchalet.com

Opposite: Belton Chalet, just outside Glacier National Park, was an architectural reminder that well-to-do tourists needn't travel to the Alps for scenery and recreation. Two guest chalets commemorate Lewis and Clark's expedition.

with easy access to the American West would no longer need to travel abroad to enjoy new vistas and glorious scenery. With buildings such as the El Tovar in the Grand Canyon, built in 1903 and heralded as a Swiss chalet with Norwegian details, designers of park lodges had already begun to make that point with architecture. At Glacier, Louis Hill envisioned a European-style system of grand hotels, backcountry camps, and chalets, a day's ride from each other on park roads and trails. He studied Swiss architecture and enlisted Spokane architects Cutter and Malmgren to develop a plan for an American alpine hostelry in harmony with its surroundings.

The Belton Chalet was the first facility the Great Northern built at Glacier, on land leased from the U.S. Forest Service, near the Belton station. The three-story chalet of milled lumber, log, rubble stone, and river rock featured a low-pitched gable roof with deep overhangs, balconies with jigsawed balustrades, and windows with lead muntins. Curved and cut corbels supporting the beams were both functional and decorative. Inside was a commodious lobby dominated by a stone fireplace, a wainscoted dining room, and ten guest rooms, furnished in the popular Arts and Crafts style. Hill also built two cabins with brick fireplaces—now dubbed "Lewis" and "Clark"—and an artist's studio. He hoped to entice scenic artist John Fery (one of his daughters was employed as the Chalet's first manager) to live at the park and paint landscapes to use in marketing, a common promotional strategy at the time. (In later years, photographers Fred H. Kiser and Tomer J. Hileman would create superb images of the park.) In 1913, the Great Northern constructed an annex featuring a long, low-pitched roof with jerkin-head gable, two levels of balconies, and twenty-four bedrooms.

But Belton had a tough time competing with the cheap tents at Lake McDonald and the swish digs at Glacier Park Lodge and Many Glacier Hotel. Despite publicity—and Minnesota waitresses attired like Swiss milkmaids—the red ink deepened, reaching flood level in the Great Depression and during World War II. In 1946, Belton Chalet was sold for less than half of its building cost. Under various owners, it became an art

Opposite: As shown in its public areas, like its lobby and snug sitting rooms, the hotel's recent restoration honored original architectural features. This page: The Chalet's decoration, which incorporates vintage Mission-style furnishings, retains the hotel's early twentieth-century character.

colony in the 1950s and a pizzeria in the 1960s. The studio was sold off, and in the 1970s the Chalet was run as a bar and restaurant with some rented rooms by Ross and Kay Luding, who owned other area lodgings.

In 1997, Belton Chalet's current owners, Cas Still and Andy Baxter, who had been in the restoration business in Florida before moving to Montana, bought the 3.5-acre property so they could spend their off-hours in the park. Over the next two years, aided by architects, landscape designers, and local contractors, they restored and renovated Belton Chalet. The goal was to install new systems and facilities without sacrificing historic integrity. Despite the property's checkered past, interiors were surprisingly intact. The annex, now the main lodge with a dining room serving "new Montana cuisine" and a cozy taproom where guests kick back in Mission Oak armchairs, was untouched for so long it was easy to replicate original paint colors, curtains, and furniture. There were tulip light fixtures, original sinks, wainscoting, and leaded windows with original glass. Sifting through decades of detritus, Baxter and Still unearthed artwork, iron beds, and oak furniture brought by train from Minnesota in 1910. They salvaged what they could and filled in the gaps with replicas and similar styles. Hanging on the walls are Edward Curtis photographs of the Blackfeet, a John Fery painting of Glacier's Highline Trail, and a photograph of Lake McDonald by Fred Kiser, found in a closet. Even the gardens were revived with native foliage, trees, and heritage lilacs, peonies, and roses. They look like they've always been there.

Members of the Blackfeet tribe still stop by, as do neighbors bearing a bit of memorabilia from the old days. The staff advises enthusiastically on wilderness activities, white-water rafting, and hiking Glacier's 730 miles of trails over and across some of the most amazing geological features in North America. But of the 150 glaciers that existed here in the nineteenth century, only thirty-five remain. The Grinnell Glacier has diminished by 90 percent, and officials believe that the park's glaciers may be gone by 2100. As Grinnell advised, take a good look, because this may already belong to the past. Or to put it another way, see Glacier first.

This page: The main lodge's dining room is a relaxing spot to relish "new Montana cuisine." Clark Cottage's sitting room is cozy. Opposite: A guest room is styled with contrasting neutrals that are easy on the eyes.

The Boulders & Golden Door Spa

There is probably more instruction-concerning-construction in the desert ways of plant life than in any books ever written.
—Frank Lloyd Wright, 1948

THE LANDSCAPE DOMINATES AT A RESORT AS UNIQUE AS ITS SETTING

How does a building begin? With an idea, even if that idea is the smallest wisp just beyond the edge of consciousness. A feeling, a visual impression, a memory, something seen, details long forgotten. After that come other ideas: an exterior, an interior, a certain size and shape, the interplay of space and volume, the quality of light on a wall. Sometimes those things are connected to a particular setting and how the building fits that setting. Where exactly will it sit? What direction will it face? What will surround it? What will people want to see and what should be hidden, and why? What will its material be, and why? What views will its windows frame?

In the early 1980s, when entrepreneur Rusty Lyon bought 1,300 acres in the Arizona desert and decided to build a resort more than an hour away from the nearest airport, hardheaded experts in the hotel business told him it was a foolhardy proposition—no one would want to go there. Lyon, ever one to sail by his own lights, thought otherwise. He hired two thirtysomething architects who had only one other hotel design to their credit. Ken Allen and Mark Philp, of Scottsdale firm Allen + Philp, visited the site with their associate Bob Bacon, charetted the idea over a long weekend, worked up some sketches, and made their presentation.

The site, in the Sonoran Desert foothills near Scottsdale, had piles of huge twelve-million-year-old granite boulders surrounded by cacti, mesquite, and scrub. Grayish-green jojoba, an evergreen and therefore a rarity in the desert, clustered about the granite rocks, which channeled runnels of rain to its thirsty

Opposite: Casitas at the Boulders Resort in Carefree, Arizona, nestle into the dramatically sculptural twelve-million-year-old granite boulders that dominate the site. The resort's building guidelines ensure that homes surrounding it are compatible with the landscape.

roots. Populated by deer, jackrabbits, and coyotes, the place was pristine. Since those boulder formations—the site's dominant, powerful feature—weren't going anywhere, there were two architectural choices. The first, to build something that complemented them; the second, to build something in contrast.

For Lyon and his architects, who loved the drama of the boulders in the desert, it wasn't really much of a choice. To complement the granite rocks and take full advantage of their sculptural strength, the shapes of the buildings needed to be simple. To harmonize with the flow of space between the formations, the relationship between the structures and the boulders was critical, and the buildings needed to follow the contour of the land.

The design team produced drawing after drawing of the site, then walked through it with the contractor, drawing the footprints of the buildings in the dirt. When they did, they saw that the largest one needed to sit twenty-five feet from where they had envisioned it. Because the boulders were the project's visual touchstone, the massing of the walls was important. Because of their massing, the buildings seem to reference the adobe structures of the desert Southwest, though the architects didn't start with the idea of building in the adobe tradition. Like the flow of the rock itself, the walls and roofs of the buildings warp into each other, a novel concept at the time. With architects as midwives, the site gave birth to the buildings.

But it did more than that. It also demanded that construction activity minimize damage to plant life that in this environment would take a long time to regrow. It dictated the layout of roads and building materials. To emphasize its drama, the road into the resort hooks through the landscape and meets the main building head-on. To show nature to its full advantage, building materials present surfaces and hues compatible with the landscape. The use of natural wood, steel, stucco, and flagstone—mostly regional materials—also helped to keep costs down. To minimize visual intrusions, Lyon readily approved the extra expense to bury power lines. Parking lots were placed at a distance, and lanes and walkways throughout the resort double as service

The Boulders & Golden Door Spa
34631 North Tom Darlington Drive
P.O. Box 2090
Carefree, AZ 85377
800-553-1717
www.wyndham.com

roads. Resort guests drive to the front entrance, and after that they have vehicle visitation rights, but there's no need for automobile transport.

Twenty years later, the Boulders is still that way. And—expert advisors hear this—the resort was an early and continuing success. With 160 guest casitas and fifty-five one-, two-, and three-bedroom pueblo villas, the Boulders is not small. But by virtue of its architecture, it feels intimate and personal, like a hideaway. Most important for future development, Lyon and the resort's other founders put design guidelines in place for private houses to be built on the site, ensuring visual consistency and sensitivity to the desert surroundings well into the future. While other resorts with private homesites suffer from architectural faux pas and grapple with this problem, the Boulders seems downright visionary. Its building guidelines have not impeded the development of private homesites, and may have increased its appeal to buyers.

Tucked into the desert terrain and colored in desert hues like the main building, the casitas and villas feature hand-hewn wood-beamed ceilings, wood-burning fireplaces stocked with fragrant mesquite logs, and Mexican tiles. Comforts include overstuffed leather chairs, high-speed Internet access, and private patios or decks overlooking the desert or golf course. The pueblo villas, a likely choice for families and groups, have fully equipped kitchens, laundry rooms, and garages.

Golf is one reason a lot of people come to the Boulders. Its two eighteen-hole championship courses were designed by Jay Morrish and are considered among the country's most challenging. The Boulders Golf Club routinely alternates use so that one course is available to its guests, while the other is kept private. Built into the desert foothills, they are distinguished by indigenous landscaping that encourages jackrabbits and rock squirrels to play in the rough. The rule on the courses, laughingly applied, is that if a player's ball goes missing and there's convincing evidence a coyote took it, the player can—without penalty—replace it with a new ball in the same spot. Though it may not help them with the coyotes, players can improve their full swing, chipping, pitching, putting, and sand techniques in individual and small-group lessons taught by PGA and

Opposite: The spa building and labyrinth and Boulder Lodge. This page: Boulders' Golden Door Spa incorporates rounded lines and Asian influences, such as a front door modeled on a Japanese temple gate.

LPGA instructors. The resort will arrange tournaments for groups of eight or more.

Those who prefer to see wildlife elsewhere than on a golf course can hike, mountain bike, horseback ride, and rock climb in North America's hottest and only tropical desert. Covering about 120,000 square miles from Baja through parts of Mexico, California, and Arizona, the Sonoran Desert has more than 600 vertebrate species, including Gila monsters, and nearly 2,300 species of perennial plants, the greatest diversity of plant life of any desert in the world. Saguaro cacti grow only in the Sonoran Desert.

The Boulders will arrange trips into the desert and to the Grand Canyon, the Navajo Reservation, Verde Canyon, Monument Valley, Lake Powell, Nogales in Mexico, Sedona, Tucson, Phoenix, Scottsdale, and other places. Frank Lloyd Wright's Taliesin West Architectural School, which served as his home and studio, is within easy reach by car.

Car? Activities at the Boulders are so tempting that cars may not only be out of sight but also out of mind. Besides golf there's tennis, with eight courts, private lessons, clinics, racket rentals, a ball machine, and 24-hour stringing and regripping services. There are galleries and shops, a Native American art museum, and eight or so cafés and restaurants, including the Latilla for gourmet regional cuisine. The Discovery Lounge, with its spectacular views of the boulder formations, is a great place to end the day.

For unwinding during the day, there's the new 33,000-square-foot Golden Door Spa designed by Newport Beach firm Wimberley, Allison, Tong & Goo. Founded in 1958, the original Golden Door, in Escondido, California, is the doyenne of American spas. This one has a huge selection of treatments, yoga, Tai Chi, Pilates, spinning, step aerobics, and kickboxing. Guests swim laps or splash in the pool, soak in a Japanese *o-furo*, take steam and Swiss showers, and enjoy a whirlpool or Watsu aquatic therapy.

Outside the lobby, water flows down the face of a granite boulder in the desert, just as it did when the architects and owners first visited the site.

This page: Interiors of the guest villas and the casitas are appointed with Asian and Southwestern details, including *viga* ceilings, tile flooring, and traditional fireplaces. Opposite: The Boulders' Latilla dining room.

Bright Angel Lodge & Phantom Ranch

On reaching the brink the whole gorge for miles lay beneath us, and it was by far the most awfully grand and impressive scene that I have ever yet seen. A suppressed sort of roar comes up constantly from the chasm but with that exception, everything impresses you with an awful stillness.
—Thomas Moran, 1873

TWO TREASURES OF THE GRAND CANYON

When Mary Elizabeth Jane Colter, one of America's first female architects, was growing up in St. Paul, Minnesota, a friend of her father gave the family a set of drawings by Sioux warriors who had fought at the Battle of Little Big Horn. She kept them all her life and referred to them as her "most priceless and precious possession." Colter found her muse early on.

In 1890, the year Colter completed her training at the California School of Design, the U.S. Census listed only twenty-two women architects. Women back then were discouraged from entering male-dominated professions. But interest in the American Southwest was burgeoning, and the region afforded Colter the freedom to pursue a career and to do great buildings —especially at the Grand Canyon. She drew upon Native American art for inspiration throughout her career, which lasted forty-six years until her retirement in 1948 at the age of seventy-nine.

Colter was born the year the canyon was named— by Major John Wesley Powell, who took nine men in four stout boats down the Colorado River in 1869, one of the explorations that opened the West. Colter would have shared his interests: A conservationist and supporter of Native American rights, Powell went on to become director of the U.S. Geological Survey and founded the U.S. Bureau of American Ethnology. In 1873, artist Thomas Moran visited the canyon with Powell and made more than thirty pieces of artwork for Powell's report and over two dozen wood

engravings to illustrate articles the explorer wrote for *Scribner's Monthly.* Moran's massive *Chasm of the Colorado,* painted after that 1873 trip, hangs in the U.S. Capitol. In 1892, to promote tourism on its lines, the Santa Fe Railroad nationally distributed thousands of full-color lithographs of Moran's *The Grand Canyon of the Colorado.* Moran's work helped make the West an integral part of American consciousness.

Colter headed west in 1902, hired by the Santa Fe Railroad and its concessionaire, the Fred Harvey Company. The Harvey Company had already established an American Indian department to source and sell native arts and was interested in site-inspired designs for its hotels. Colter's first project was to design interiors for the Indian Building, part of the Alvarado Hotel designed by Charles Whittelsey in Albuquerque, New Mexico. A new concept, the building contained sales space, a museum, and demonstration areas. Colter devised theme rooms, including a Navajo room with blanketed walls, pottery, and baskets, and a Spanish and Mexican room—all full of home-decorating merchandise that could be purchased and shipped.

In 1904, three years after the first passenger train arrived at the Grand Canyon, Harvey asked Colter to work there. She made her debut as an architect with Hopi House, a sales and exhibit center near El Tovar. Colter re-created Hopi dwellings at Oraibi, Arizona, the oldest inhabited community in the United States, employing Hopi craftsmen who built Hopi House using stone and adobe with layered timber-thatched ceilings. Hopi House showcased Native American arts, and included a space for Hopi artisans to work. Colter's next projects were Hermit's Rest and Lookout Studio, structures of piled rock and logs that follow the contours of their sites and seem to be land formations rather than buildings.

Hopi House, Hermit's Rest, and Lookout Studio, still among the most visited sites in the park, show how Colter—a contemporary of Frank Lloyd Wright— forged her own path, with site-inspired buildings that referenced history, relied on natural materials, and, in their irregularity, imitated the work of nature.

Bright Angel Lodge &
Phantom Ranch
Grand Canyon National Park,
South Rim
Xanterra Parks & Resorts
Grand Canyon, AZ 86023
888-297-2757
www.grandcanyonlodges.com

Opposite: Architect Mary Colter, born in 1869, the year the Grand Canyon was named, took her inspiration for Bright Angel Lodge and cabins, on the canyon's much-visited south rim, from vernacular buildings of the Southwest.

For inspiration, she visited archaeological sites and studied Indian cultures. She neither had nor needed an architectural license: Based on her concepts, floor plans, and elevations, the Santa Fe Railroad's architects and engineers completed working drawings. Though she was little known, Colter's environmentally sensitive designs, completely consistent with park policy of minimal disruption of nature, helped to define the architectural style that came to be known as "national park rustic" and were influential in and outside the park system.

In 1917, shortly after the creation of the National Park Service, officials developed a plan for the Grand Canyon, stating that "no permit for an unnecessarily ugly or objectionable building should be issued anywhere for any purpose." The National Park Service's first director, Stephen Mather, said, "Particular attention must be devoted always to harmonizing of [park] improvements with the landscape." And park planners wrote, "As long as the company's work is passed upon to Miss Colter, its present architect, [the appropriateness of their buildings] can be considered assured." The Harvey and Santa Fe interests agreed. Colter, now Harvey's chief designer, developed a plan for future buildings, roads, trails, and landscaped areas that governed development of the south rim into the 1940s.

In 1922, Colter again demonstrated her design philosophy with the construction of Phantom Ranch, lodging for those who descended the canyon to Bright Angel Creek. On the rim of the canyon, visitors are awed by its vast, sweeping majesty, but to descend a mile down through its ancient geology, to see the view Powell saw when he first explored it, instills humility. In 1921, the National Park Service began improvements of the trail to the canyon floor, and asked the Harvey Company to build tourist accommodations on Bright Angel Creek about a quarter of a mile from where it meets the Colorado River. In 1922, on a site that had been a rough camp for hunters and tourists since 1907, Colter built a small complex: four cabins, a cabin for a caretaker, and a lodge housing a kitchen and dining room. Stones from the site were laid, boulders at the bottom, to form foundations, walls, and chimneys. Pack mules brought all the other building materials—wood posts for framing, window sash and doors, and decorative elements—across a wobbly suspension bridge and down the rocky trails. The buildings' gable roofs were low-pitched, and the exteriors

took their green, reddish, and brown color schemes from nature. Inside, each building has a stone fireplace and a concrete tile floor, and their original decoration featured primary colors and Indian rugs. Colter called the place Phantom Ranch after a nearby canyon, so named because it was so narrow that it seemed to disappear from view. The facility was expanded several times, including a 1927–28 expansion that Colter supervised. Because of its design, building materials, and coloration and the grove of cottonwood trees that has grown up around it, Phantom Ranch disappears into the landscape. The only means of access remain mule, foot, and boat, and reservations for its mostly dormitory-style accommodations are made up to two years in advance.

After building Phantom Ranch, Colter's work took her away from the Grand Canyon, but she returned in 1932 to design the seventy-foot-high Watchtower, an imagined Anasazi structure with a concrete foundation and a concealed steel frame.

The National Park Service was concerned about Bright Angel Hotel, an unsightly sprawl of cabins and tents, as early as 1917. It wanted "a group of artistic and plain, but clean and light housekeeping cottages." The eyesore was razed, and on a rocky rise along the rim promenade, Colter built its replacement. A 1934 National Park Service report called Bright Angel Lodge an innovation in park construction. "In their rambling one-story design," it said, "the buildings suggest an interesting little village which has gradu-

Opposite: Colter, on right, shows plans for Bright Angel. The lodge's lobby celebrates Native American craftsmanship and features a "geologic fireplace" replicating the canyon's rock strata. Guest cabins seem a step back in time. This page: Grand Canyon, winter.

ally grown up on the rim of the canyon." The cabins themselves are not hidden away—they are right on the path along the rim, and at some times of day during heavily touristed weekends and vacations, there's foot traffic thirty feet from one's window. But during quiet times—just at sunrise, for instance—it would be hard to find a better view, and the cabins feel secluded, especially to city folk who like the civility of being in the Grand Canyon village.

Colter created the impression of a little village with her approach to massing and choice of materials. Each of Bright Angel's cottages is different. Viga-studded adobe, board and batten siding, logs, rough stone, and varied clapboards and shingles define the exteriors. Several cabins feature multiple-shed roofs

in pinwheel formation—something modernist architects did too, but in Colter's hands, they are firmly rooted in a vernacular tradition. The ranchlike lodge has a main portico with stripped log columns, a lobby featuring log and plank construction, flagstone flooring, and a fireplace of Kaibab limestone surmounted by a painted and feathered thunderbird, a Harvey Company trademark. The star of the building is its "geological fireplace," layered stone replicating the rock strata in the canyon, from the smooth stones of the Colorado River to the Kaibab limestone at the rim. For the interiors, Colter used comfortable rustic furnishings, Western and Native American motifs, and a unifying color workmen called "Mary Jane blue."

As an admirer of historic buildings, Colter saved

two relics of earlier days from demolition by the National Park Service when she designed Bright Angel Lodge. One is Red Horse Station, built in the 1890s as a stagecoach stop and moved in 1902 to the Grand Canyon village. It is now a two-room cabin, with pegged oak flooring and chinked log ceilings and walls. The other is a log cabin built in 1896 by William "Buckey" O'Neill, an author, miner, politician, and judge who discovered copper deposit in the canyon but found that the cost of shipping ore made mining unprofitable. (O'Neill went on to become mayor of Prescott, Arizona, and joined Theodore Roosevelt's Rough Riders in Cuba, where he was killed the day before the charge up San Juan Hill.) In the 1930s, Colter made these two buildings part of Bright Angel Lodge.

Bright Angel Lodge now comprises a total of eighty-nine rooms in its main registration building and eighteen cabins and dormitory-style accommodations. These include thirty-five rooms in sixteen historic wood-and-stucco buildings ranging from one to four rooms in size. Fifteen of these are on the canyon rim, four have fireplaces, and two (numbers 6151 and 6152) have both fireplaces and spectacular views of the canyon. Bright Angel's most deluxe suite is the one in the Buckey O'Neill cabin. The lodge's family-style restaurant serves breakfast, lunch, and dinner; its Arizona Room serves up Southwestern cuisine and excellent steaks.

Phantom Ranch, the only lodging at the bottom of the canyon, offers accommodations in rustic stone cabins and in gender-segregated dormitories. It has a canteen and can serve up a steak dinner, providing it's ordered when making reservations.

Bright Angel Lodge and Phantom Ranch are the two end points of the trails linking the canyon rim and floor, and Bright Angel is the departure point for the bumpy, sometimes spine-jarring mule rides down into the canyon. But waking before sunrise in either place, people experience the same awesome views and stillness that Powell and Moran did more than 200 years ago. That's a long time in human terms, but a very brief one here.

This page: There's horseback riding on the rim, but visitors usually travel the rugged path to the base of the Canyon by mule. Opposite: Phantom Ranch, designed by Mary Colter, is the only lodging inside the canyon.

Cibolo Creek Ranch

... in the west a few fleecy clouds, gorgeously golden for a fleeting instant, then crimson-crowned for another, shaded and darkened as the setting sun sank behind the hills. Presently... a pink glow suffused the heavens, and at last, as gray twilight stole down over the hilltops, the crescent moon (appeared)....
—Zane Grey, *The Spirit of the Border*, 1906

RESTORATION AND RELAXATION
WEST OF THE PECOS

This scene has repeated itself night after night in Big Bend country since time immemorial. It's the same one seen by the Indians whom the Spanish called "Cibolo," meaning "buffalo," who camped here just as their ancestors did 6,000 years ago. It was no different in 1857, when Milton Faver, one of Texas's first great cattlemen, built the three fortified buildings that comprise Cibolo Creek Ranch and fought off the Apaches to defend them. Nowadays, in the evening, the ranch's staff lights a campfire, laughingly referred to as "south Texas TV," and guests who are so inclined gather for conversation. Sitting out there, waiting for the stars to emerge in the night sky, Cibolo Creek Ranch assumes a timeless quality, like the landscape itself.

In the Big Bend country of far west Texas just twenty-six miles from the Mexican border, the Chinati Mountains define a rugged terrain of rocky peaks, sheltered canyons, and mesas rising from 4,000 to 6,000 feet in elevation. The ranch owes its existence to precious natural springs that water its livestock and orchards and keep it moist, green, and cool even when surrounding terrain is drought-dry and dusty.

Located thirty-three miles south of Marfa, Texas, just over 200 miles from the closest commercial airport and with its own 5,300-foot-long paved and lit private airstrip, Cibolo Creek Ranch is a meticulously restored collection of three mid-nineteenth-century fortifications. It is a working cattle ranch with one of the largest purebred longhorn herds in the United States. It doesn't consider itself a dude ranch, though it has a large remuda of horses that one can ride. With a group of ten people, guests can even arrange for a cattle drive, depending upon the season and the needs of the herd. The ranch also holds authentic rodeos, drawing real ranchers from both sides of the border. But what Cibolo Creek is really about is soul-satisfying serenity and solitude. The ranch's 32,000 acres offer a multitude of ways to exercise the body and mind, including a library of Texas tales, none more remarkable than that of the ranch itself.

In 1987, when Cibolo Creek's owner, Houstonian John Poindexter, first saw it, the place was "a picturesque ruin," a generous way to describe a time-ravaged study in collapsed roofs and crumbling walls, broken windows, and empty stone foundations so buried in overgrowth as to be invisible. Poindexter thought the place was a work of art. It took three years to buy it and nearly four to restore. "How often," he said, "does the opportunity appear to re-create a meaningful fragment of the historical life of a region, particularly one so physically and romantically attractive as the Big Bend?"

That meaningful fragment is Milton Faver. Though barely five feet in height, Faver was a larger-than-life figure. Don Meliton, as he was locally called, was largely responsible for establishing cattle, sheep, and goat ranching as lasting economic enterprises in far west Texas, then a lawless terra incognita. Reputed to have shot a man in Missouri, Faver is said to have fled to Mexico, perhaps via the Santa Fe Trail. In any case, by 1840, at the age of about twenty, he was in Chihuahua working at a flour mill. He married a well-connected Mexican beauty and began hauling goods along the Chihuahua Trail from Mexico to Texas.

Early in his freight enterprise, Faver began supplying flour, corn, beans, sweet potatoes, and beef to Fort Davis. Named after Jefferson Davis, secretary of war in President Franklin Pierce's cabinet, the fort was established in 1854 to protect Texas settlers and pioneers headed to California. Fort Davis was the base of the 8th Infantry and the 9th and 10th Cavalries, African-American regiments that the Indians nicknamed

Cibolo Creek Ranch
HCR 67, Box 44
Marfa, TX 79843
866-496-9460
www.cibolocreekranch.com

Opposite: Fortin del Cibolo, one of three restored mid-nineteenth-century forts, now a unique hotel and working cattle ranch, in Texas Big Bend country. The original builder, Milton Faver, was one of the founders of the great cattle drives.

"Buffalo Soldiers," who were known for discharging the Army's worst assignments brilliantly.

To profit fully from his freighting venture, Faver needed to raise cattle. At that time, Big Bend country was waist-deep in fifty kinds of grass but highly vulnerable to drought. Faver shrewdly purchased 320 acres, a strategic square half-mile in the most accessible passage through the Chinati mountain range and containing Cibolo Spring, one of the most reliable and productive water sources in the region. In 1857, on a prime site bordered by a high plateau and a creek, Faver built Fortin del Cibolo. The rectangular structure consisted of two wings at right angles, with its remaining sides completed by thick adobe walls, and two two-story towers. Designed to be defensible against raiding Apaches and Mexican bandits, its roof offered no access into the building; rooms opened off into the courtyard but not into one another; one of its wings was big enough to enclose several wagons; and, from loopholes in the towers and rooms near them, rifle and pistol fire could pick off anyone scaling the walls. During one attack, an Indian tunneled into the fort; he was skewered crosswise with a sword so others couldn't pull him out or follow him in.

Shortly after building Fortin del Cibolo, Faver built Fortin de la Cienega, followed by La Morita. In 1862, Apaches routed the small Confederate force at Fort Davis, and the Indians, reclaiming their ancestral land, launched attacks against Big Bend's settlers. Most of the Anglo population left; Faver stayed. His forts were never breached.

Fortin del Cibolo was the center of the ranch's agricultural production, which included orchards of peaches, the most lucrative item Faver grew. He used to make peach brandy, which he traded to soldiers, Indians, and settlers alike, and dispensed generously in his cattle camps and home. Livestock were centered at La Cienega.

Expanding his land holdings, Faver built a herd of Texas longhorns that at one time totaled 20,000. It was, a contemporary said, "the wildest ever to set foot on the Texas range." Descended from cattle brought by Columbus to the Caribbean and by Spanish colonists to Mexico, longhorns were skilled foragers, aggressive against predators, and ideally suited to Big Bend country. In 1867, Faver was one of the founders of the Trans-Pecos cattle drives along the Chihuahua Trail, which restocked Mexico's northern ranges where herds had been decimated by Indian raids during the Civil War.

With respect for Cibolo Creek Ranch's history, Poindexter restored the three forts. To ensure accuracy he used physical evidence, including the buildings themselves and archaeological excavations, as well as documentary sources such as firsthand period accounts, oral histories, and drawings and photographs done in 1936 for the Historic American Buildings Survey, which showed long-gone features like windows and the floor plan for La Cienega.

The forts' restorers had to relearn the art of making

Opposite: A moonrise, authentic adobe bricks, a 1930s photograph restorers used, and a tower where early occupants fought Apaches, give Cibolo Creek a feeling of timelessness. This page: In a courtyard, wooden cart wheels recall frontier history.

adobe bricks. They mixed clay-rich mud with straw; in this case, a process traditionally done with the feet was accomplished with a tractor's front-end loader. This is pressed into molds that are inverted, sliding the wet bricks on the ground, where the sun hardens them. To avoid cracking, the mixture must be free of stones, and mortar must be of the same material. Finally, walls are coated with a layer of the same mud clay. (In the 1840s, federal land agents suggested adobe as a building material for prairie settlements. Obviously, it only works in a dry climate: In fact, the roof parapets on an adobe building protect the walls below from rain, and when they erode, they can be easily repaired.)

The forts' original roof and ceiling structures consisted of round ceiling beams called *vigas*, measuring up to a foot in diameter and placed about two feet apart. Between and perpendicular to them, cottonwood branches called *rajas*, a few inches wide and placed flat-side down, form the ceilings of the rooms. Over these is a layer of brush and a topmost layer of packed adobe. During restoration, the layer of brush was removed, creating space for heating, cooling, and other mechanical systems.

The project involved myriad professionals—historians, the architectural firm Ford, Powell, and Carson of San Antonio, and Hispanic laborers who proved themselves masters of many trades. It included a new guest hacienda that replicated the adobe's appearance with modern materials, miles of roadway, dry-laid stone fences, driveways, water and sewer systems, the replanting of Faver's orchards, and other landscaping. Buffalo, elk, wild turkeys, oxen, burros, and the type of camels used in the nineteenth-century Southwest by the U.S. Cavalry were reintroduced.

Inside and out, Cibolo Creek Ranch today looks very much as it would have in the 1800s. Power lines for new utilities are buried and all the systems hidden. In the guest rooms, access to the baths is concealed by a faux armoire with wooden doors.

The three historic forts, each a good distance from each other, are appointed with antique furnishings and comfortable seating, fireplaces, Saltillo tile floors, and spacious verandas. Each uniquely designed room captures the ranch's historic spirit and style. The largest fort, El Fortin del Cibolo, and its adjoining hacienda comprise twenty-two guest rooms, a living room, library, dining room, and museum rooms. El Fortin de la Cienega, across the ranch, offers three private guest rooms within the fort and seven more in its adjoining hacienda. The smallest fort, La Morita, "the mulberry tree," is an intimate two-room cottage.

Cibolo Creek Ranch prides itself on arranging personalized itineraries. On the ranch there's swimming, catch-and-release fishing, clay target shooting, mountain biking on more than one hundred miles of roads, paddle boating, bird- and bat-watching, horseback riding, and abundant wildlife. There are ruins of pioneer cabins and a ranger camp, Indian caves and ancient pictographs, a waterfall, and a spring-fed lake. Guests can explore the ranch's museums and library, rejuvenate at its spa, organize a game of billiards, watch TV in one of the common spaces, or steal a few hours to work in its guest office. The impeccable nineteenth-century restoration includes twenty-first-century amenities.

Off the ranch, there's rafting on the Rio Grande and easy access to Big Bend National Park, Big Bend Ranch State Park, the Black Gap Wildlife Management Area, and Davis Mountains State Park. The McDonald Observatory, the world's best-equipped; Fort Davis and Fort Leaton historic sites; and the silver mining town of Shafter, now a ghost town, are also nearby. The ranch is located just twenty minutes from a U.S. entry point into Mexico.

As it did in Faver's day, the ranch retains the atmosphere of a border enterprise. Many of its staff are Hispanic and bilingual. Its wonderful dining room offers venison, buffalo, wild boar, rib-eye steaks, pecans, citrus, and farm-raised shrimp from Texas, along with some of Mexico's finest corn tortillas, beers, papaya, oregano, and vanilla used to flavor desserts. Guests usually don't want to be far away when the dinner bell rings.

Cibolo Creek Ranch even offers archery for children, provided they are supervised. This activity can be served up with a lesson in history: One elderly Marfa resident recalls the day in her childhood when she picked bucketsful of Apache arrowheads from the walls of El Fortin del Cibolo.

Opposite: Cibolo Creek Ranch's historic stone walls now encompass a swimming pool. It—and the green terrain—are reminders that this site contains one of the most prolific natural springs in this part of Texas.

Dunton Hot Springs

That night we camped beside a spring that flowed fresh and bright from the tender grass and was a gift to our tired horses. The spot was surrounded by bushes and trees.... The Apache chief stationed two sentinels, and everything seemed to assure our safety as we sat around the fire.

—translated from Karl May's *The Treasure of Nugget Mountain*, 1898

A GHOST TOWN RESURRECTED AS A LUXE RETREAT IN THE COLORADO WILDS

Thirty miles south of Telluride, 8,900 feet above sea level, in the shadow of Colorado's Mount Wilson—really, in the middle of nowhere—geothermal springs send ribbons of steam into the pristine air. It's not German writer Karl May's *The Treasure of Nugget Mountain,* but it might pass for that. Gold, silver, and lead were what the miners came for in the 1890s, when the Smuggler and Emma mining companies established the town of Dunton, Colorado. Here, twenty-two miles up the West Fork of the Dolores River, in a sweet spot surrounded by mountain meadows, sweeping stands of aspen, and 14,000-foot mountain peaks, they built a post office, general store, school, cabins to house the miners, an iron forge, a saloon, a brothel, and a church—to counteract the influence of the brothel and the saloon. Dunton grew to a population of 500 souls.

After the mines played out and the town was abandoned in 1918, three brothers bought Dunton and turned it into a low-key dude ranch. It changed hands a few times but remained a resort until 1973, when absentee ownership and later unsavory business deals left the place wide open for trouble. Trouble came in the form of gun-toting, liquor-swilling motorcycle gangs, hippies, runaways, and desperadoes. Lawlessness ruled. By 1990 the cabins had turned into shacks, and barely that. Dunton had become a ghost town.

Four years later, Austrian Bernt Kuhlmann and German Christoph Henkel walked across the Dolores River Bridge and fell in love with the place. They were not the first Europeans to be entranced by the American West. Early in the nineteenth century, German prince Maximilian zu Weid's 1832–34 expedition to the frontier included Swiss artist Karl Bodmer, one of the first artists to render images of Native Americans on canvas. Many Europeans returned home with souvenirs that form some fine collections of Native American art and artifacts, including the one in the Karl May Museum in Radebeul, Germany.

Kuhlmann, who had been working in real estate and dreaming of developing a ghost town, had spent his boyhood reading novels by May, the turn-of-the-century German writer who penned vivid, best-selling tales of the American West without ever having been there. Henkel, scion of a family that made its fortune in consumer products, spent his childhood summers in a Tyrolean hunting cabin and had recently purchased a ranch near Telluride. The two, who met while working in the film industry in Los Angeles, looked past the broken windows and caved-in roofs, mice under the floorboards, and a bathhouse riddled with bullet holes and bought Dunton with the idea of turning it into a bachelor pad.

They found Native American craftsmen to restore the hand-hewn log buildings. To replace the cabins that were past saving, Kuhlmann searched five states, found eight authentic period substitutes, had them dismantled, trucked in, and rebuilt with twenty-first-century comforts such as radiant underfloor heat and smoked-glass showers.

Dunton didn't remain a private bachelor pad for long. For one thing, both Kuhlmann and Henkel got married. And they realized that their considerable investment demanded a return, so they began hosting corporate retreats, then accepted paying guests. Dunton was, as Henkel says, "a private place too large for a private family." Today, guests can rent individual cabins or the entire town.

Dunton Hot Springs has eleven authentic hand-hewn log cabins, accommodating some twenty-eight

Dunton Hot Springs
P.O. Box 818
Dolores, CO 81323
970-882-4800
www.duntonhotsprings.com

Opposite: Outside Telluride, Colorado, a collection of vintage cabins, some original to this mining site and some imported and reconstructed, was arrayed around mineral springs and baths to create a retreat like no other. A massive tepee tents a hot spring.

guests. Each cabin has a singular character and history. The interiors are warmed by wood stoves and furnished for comfort. One boasts its own private hot spring and a tin tub in which to cool off. The decor is varied but uniformly and fashionably rustic, ranging from Navajo textiles and artifacts to kilims, bearskin rugs, elk-hide bedspreads, leather armchairs, and antique furniture, including an eighteenth-century bedstead from Rajasthan, India.

Within walking distance of the cabins are a massive tepee tenting one hot spring; a rocky geothermal pool for soaking alfresco; the main bathhouse, which features a hot spring pool, steam room, shower room, and massage loft; open-air church; a vintage barn from Durango containing the library; a Pony Express Stop from the nearby town of Parachute that serves as a yoga studio; and the saloon, which comprises a conference facility and a dining room. Being a saloon, it of course also has a bar, with generations of graffiti, including "Butch Cassidy + Sundance Kid." As legend has it, the two outlaws, fired from jobs building the railroad to Salt Lake City, had just robbed their first bank—in Telluride—and chose Dunton to hide out in. The initials may or may not be bogus—it hardly matters. Dunton is a hideout—and a luxe one—for writers, publishers, fashion editors and designers, film people, and princesses by birth and otherwise.

Since the historic days, when mule trains brought

Opposite: Thermal springs are outside and inside the bathhouse. This page: Dunton's rustic saloon was a desperado's haven in the '70s and before. Butch Cassidy and the Sundance Kid allegedly carved their names in the vintage bar.

melons, tomatoes, chilies, corn, and peaches up the trails from McElmo Canyon, the area's bread basket, Dunton has had a tradition of fine food. Its chef goes to great lengths to obtain the freshest, highest-quality local ingredients from McElmo and elsewhere. Nowadays, the menu at Dunton Hot Springs might include world-famous Olanthe sweet corn, Grand Champion beef, elk with lingonberries, truffle omelettes, locally harvested chanterelles, and wines from Dunton's impressive cellar.

Travel the road to Dunton (the last nine miles are unpaved) and you can turn your bones to jelly in one of the resort's three 103-degree spring-fed baths, while enjoying the intoxicating effect of the lithium-laced waters. Or, with the caution dictated by the altitude, you can kick back with Dickel "sippin' whiskey" that Henkel calls "the unofficial beverage of the West Fork." Or, you can ease into more active pursuits, starting with what the staff calls "extreme picnicking."

In winter, there's snowshoeing, snowmobiling, cross-country skiing, and heli-skiing, with a 'copter that obligingly lands in front of the saloon. If a blizzard renders people snowbound, there's the consolation of the saloon and the hot springs. In summer, there's hiking to a thirty-five-foot waterfall and in a national forest, wine tasting at nearby Sutcliffe Vineyards, horseback riding, mountain biking, mountain climbing, white-water rafting, kayaking, creek boating, and fly-fishing in the Dolores River, or, for guests yearning for a more manicured landscape, golf in Telluride or Cortez. Native American sites include the Mesa Verde Center of the Anasazi civilization, a museum and working archaeological site, just ninety minutes to the southwest. Guests flying in via Denver can visit the Denver Art Museum's world-class collection of Native American art and artifacts.

Although mobile phones are not an option here, type A types will be comforted by the knowledge that telephones and wireless Internet access are available. Of course, at Dunton, one might change one's view about that. It's all too tempting—aside from enjoying the conviviality of the other guests—to go for miles into the wilderness and not see or hear another soul.

This page: Accommodations in the tepee include a kilim rug and a bearskin. Opposite: Decoration in Dunton's library harks back to the days of Teddy Roosevelt. Three guest rooms show chinked log construction and Western mountain style at its most interesting.

El Tovar

Grand Canyon is the grandest of all canyons because at that particular place all the necessary conditions were fulfilled more exuberantly than at any other place in the whole world.
—Joseph Wood Krutch, *The Voice of the Desert: A Naturalist's Interpretation*, 1955

A GRAND HOTEL OVERLOOKING THE WORLD'S GRANDEST CANYON

There are only seven wonders of the natural world. El Tovar, an architectural gem of the U.S. National Park system, commands the south rim of one of them—an ancient river-carved chasm, measuring 277 miles long, four to eighteen miles wide, and more than a mile deep. It is one place where the word "awesome" truly has meaning.

The Grand Canyon, displaying more than half of the earth's 4.6-billion-year history, has been called a geological museum of epic proportions. About seventy million years ago, a tectonic shift formed the Rocky Mountains and raised an area of the American Southwest measuring about 130,000 square miles from below sea level to thousands of feet. Over the next five or six million years, the sediment-laden ancestors of the Colorado River deepened and widened the canyon. Erosion exposed rock strata that range from the 1.7-billion-year-old Vishnu Schist of the Inner Gorge and Kaibab limestone deposited 250 million years ago to the 1,000 to several-million-year-old black-lava flows in the western canyon. Human history in this ancient geology began 10,000 years ago. First came Paleolithic hunters, then hunter-gatherers, who were succeeded by agricultural societies, and, by A.D. 500, the Anasazi, ancestors of the modern Pueblo Indians. In 1857, a U.S. Army survey, led by Lieutenant Joseph Ives, came to map the canyon. Ives wrote, "The region is . . . of course altogether valueless. . . . Ours has been the first, and will doubtless be the last,

party of whites to visit this profitless locality."

By the 1870s, this "profitless" hole in the desert was being mined for zinc, copper, lead, and asbestos. The canyon's first settler, John Hance, arrived in 1883 to mine asbestos. But the canyon's greatest value is its capacity to inspire. Tourists came, attracted by reports and illustrations of its wonders.

To protect the canyon, in 1882, then-Senator Benjamin Harrison introduced unsuccessful legislation to make it a national park. Eleven years later, as president, he named it a national forest reserve. In 1906, President Theodore Roosevelt, who had visited the canyon with John Muir, designated it a game preserve. Two years later, to ensure its protection from developers, Roosevelt, by presidential proclamation, set aside 800,000 acres as the Grand Canyon National Monument. "In the Grand Canyon," he said, "Arizona has a natural wonder which, so far as I know, is in kind absolutely unparalleled throughout the rest of the world. . . . Keep this great wonder of nature as it is. . . . You cannot improve it. The ages have been at work on it, and man can only mar it. Keep it for your children and your children's children, and for all who come after you, as one of the great sights which every American, if he can travel at all, must see." Finally, in 1919, Congress established the Grand Canyon as a national park. Today, the park totals more than 1.2 million acres.

The Santa Fe Railroad opened train service to the park in 1901, and in 1903, to accommodate tourists, it commissioned Illinois architect Charles Whittlesey to design a first-class luxury hotel. Whittlesey, who had trained in Louis Sullivan's Chicago office and designed the railroad's mission-style Alvarado Hotel in Albuquerque, New Mexico, conceived of El Tovar—named after the Spanish explorer who dispatched the first group of Europeans to reach the canyon—as an elegant hunting lodge.

Built of huge Oregon pine shipped by rail, the hotel rises four stories from a rough limestone base to a mansard roof. It features log walls, beams, and

El Tovar
Grand Canyon National Park, South Rim
Xanterra Parks & Resorts
Grand Canyon, AZ 86023
888-297-2757
www.grandcanyonlodges.com

Opposite: El Tovar, built in the manner of a stylish European hunting lodge, hugs the south rim of the Grand Canyon, as it has since the Santa Fe Railroad—and Model T's—first began bringing visitors here in 1905.

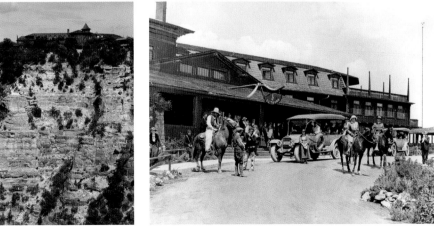

columns; Norwegian-style cutout railings; wide verandas; recessed window seats; and arches and fireplaces built of native stone. In the days when luxury simply meant electric lighting and indoor plumbing, El Tovar was equipped with a coal-fired steam generator, and its distinctive tower housed a large metal water tank. It had a central rotunda lobby, solarium, music and amusement rooms, bar, wicker-filled sun parlor, and an eighty-nine-foot-long dining room, and it was appointed with Gustav Stickley furnishings and Native American and Western art. When it opened in 1905, at a final cost of $250,000, El Tovar was, one newspaper said, "the most expensively constructed and appointed log house in America."

Whittlesey was wise enough to know that no mere building could compete with the grandeur of the Grand Canyon, so he chose to create lodge architecture on a grand scale twenty feet from the rim, offering guests what they really came for: "the surprise of the supreme moment" when they viewed the canyon. The result was an enormously influential building—one of the national park structures that inspired a building tradition wryly called "Parkitecture."

El Tovar has been remodeled several times but

This page and opposite: Decorations in "the most expensively constructed and appointed log house in America" include Arts and Crafts furniture and paintings by Western artists. Amid tourist throngs, guests hide away in the hotel's many nooks and crannies.

has retained its original character. Even though the canyon's south rim gets some four million visitors a year and the hotel sits in the middle of the action, its nooks and crannies afford escape from the madding crowds. It now offers sixty-six guest rooms, each with a private bath, and twelve suites, some with canyon views; fine regional cuisine in the famous dining room; and an intimate place to gather in the lounge. Reservations are often made two years in advance. But the hotel's story doesn't end with architecture.

The hotel's first concessionaire was Fred Harvey, an English immigrant who came to America in 1850 at the age of fifteen and worked in a variety of railroad restaurants. Appalled at the poor quality that was the norm, Harvey decided there was a market for first-class food, service, and cleanliness at reasonable prices. He opened the first Harvey House in Topeka, Kansas, in 1876, and in 1878, entered a partnership with the Atchison, Topeka, and Santa Fe Railroad. By 1889 he had earned exclusive rights to operate restaurants, lunch stands, and hotels on all the railroad's lines west of the Missouri River.

Harvey originated the gourmet cuisine in El Tovar's dining room. Persian melons, Camembert, fresh Pacific salmon, Kansas beef, California oranges for fresh-squeezed juice, and spring water for coffee were brought 120 miles daily by rail. But what distinguished all Harvey Company establishments was the staff—called "Harvey Girls"—who set a national standard for customer service. Outfitted in starched black dresses with white collars and aprons, these "young women, 18 to 30 years of age, of good character, attractive and intelligent," were governed by strict rules of behavior on and off the job. Many married locally, becoming the founding mothers of Western towns. Their story was told in the 1946 film *The Harvey Girls,* starring Angela Lansbury and Judy Garland, who sang "The Atchison, Topeka, and Santa Fe."

Nowadays people can view the canyon by plane and helicopter, or explore its geology by foot, horse, or mule, and some guests still hum that tune on the Grand Canyon Railway's scenic tours.

This page: Native American motifs add impact to El Tovar's dining room, originally staffed by Harvey Girls, employed by the Santa Fe Railroad's concessionaire and known for their impeccable service. Opposite: Guest rooms reflect the hotel's historic character.

Emerald Lake Lodge

When the train . . . has puffed through the spiral tunnels below the peaks . . . (and) when you have come . . . across the river and through that glorious arcade of slender jack pines . . . beside the rippling, green water, with a shining mountain ridge behind you, then only have you found the threshold of true contentment.

—J. Monroe Thorington, *The Glittering Mountains of Canada*, 1925

A THRESHOLD OF TRUE CONTENTMENT IN THE CANADIAN ROCKIES

Tom Wilson was led to Emerald Lake in 1882. A railway surveyor, he was exploring the Canadian Rockies. The terrain was rough and hard on the ponies he had bought from some Indian friends, so he left some spare horses to rest while he went on. When he returned to the mountain pasture where he'd left them, the horses were gone. He followed their tracks west along Kicking Horse River, across streams, and along rough, forested trails. Finally, in a hidden valley that the Shuswap and Ktunaxa Indians used to avoid their enemies, the Blackfoot (as the Blackfeet tribe is known in Canada), he found the ponies on the shore of one of the most breathtaking lakes he'd ever see in a lifelong career as a guide and outfitter. Wilson never claimed to have discovered Emerald Lake; Native Americans had done that long before, and their horses led him to it.

When guests travel the six-mile road leading to Emerald Lake Lodge, they are on the trail, now widened and paved, that Wilson's Indian ponies followed in 1882.

By 1884, the Canadian Pacific Railway had advanced through the slough where Wilson had pastured his horses, to Field, the town closest to the Emerald Lake Lodge, where the railway established a maintenance center and opened the Mount Stephen

Opposite: In winter, the Canadian Rockies are a snow lover's dream, especially when the powder is chin deep. The lodge is a starting point for cross-country skiers, and downhill skiing is nearby. By night, its windows glow with welcoming light.

House, a hotel and restaurant that helped the railroad avoid hauling heavy dining cars up through Kicking Horse Pass. In 1886, the Canadian government set aside the mountain landscape on the western side of the Great Divide as a reserve. Emerald Lake soon became one of the area's most popular tourist attractions. The idea for a hotel came later, from Edward Whymper. Nicknamed "Lion of the Matterhorn," Whymper had been the first to conquer the great Swiss peak in 1865, but in an accident that stunned Europe, four men fell 4,000 feet to their deaths, and people talked of banning climbing. Even so, all of Europe's peaks were conquered by 1885, the year the Canadian Pacific finished laying track—and announced there were 1,100 unclimbed peaks in the Canadian West. To promote mountaineering, the railway hired Swiss mountain guides and invited Whymper. The lodging at Emerald Lake, built by the railway on land in Yoho National Park, was one of his recommendations.

The original building at Emerald Lake was designed by the railway's chief architect, Thomas Sorby, as a summer getaway in the Swiss rustic tradition. The chalet, of hewn timber with stone and hardwood interiors, had fourteen bedrooms and a dining room. Opened in 1902, Emerald Lake Chalet immediately became a popular access point to the upper reaches of the Yoho Valley. By 1906, it had been expanded twice and included six cabins designed by the railway's architect, Francis Rattenbury. Early guests included botanists Dr. Charles and Mary Schaeffer, poet Rudyard Kipling, and, in 1907, American geologist Charles Dolittle Walcott, Secretary of the Smithsonian Institution, who founded the Burgess Pass Fossil Quarry above Emerald Lake. The Quarry contains the 530-million-year-old remains of 150 species of Mid-Cambrian marine creatures. Among the earliest forms of life on earth, they were deposited some 400 million years before tectonic shifts formed the Rockies.

By the mid-1920s, mass-produced Ford touring cars were bringing the masses. The chalet was expanded in 1924, and again in 1932 to a total of thirty

Emerald Lake Lodge
P.O. Box 10
Field, British Columbia, Canada
V0A 1G0
800-663-6336
www.emeraldlakelodge.com

cabins around the main chalet, accommodating 120 guests. But during the Great Depression and World War II, tourism dropped. New motels serving automobile tourists siphoned business from the park lodges. By the 1950s, Emerald Lake Chalet was a losing enterprise, its buildings dated and in need of repair. In 1959, the Canadian Pacific Railway sold two properties: Emerald Lake Chalet, to the Brewster Transport Company of Banff, and Moraine Lake Lodge, to Bill and Barbara Smyth, who narrowly missed the chance to buy Emerald Lake Chalet. In 1965, the chance came again, and they took it. Seven years later, they sold the chalet to a young Dutch couple, Frances and Bob Holscher, who met while attending hotel school and brought a European standard of professional service. By the late 1970s, the physical plant needed extensive work, and the chalet was sold again—this time to

a group of partners. Among them was businessman John O'Connor, whose parents had ridden horseback to Emerald Lake on their honeymoon.

Almost immediately, Parks Canada ordered the property closed, because its dated diesel-powered electric generator and water and sewage systems had become a threat to the lake; it also ordered some of the leased land to be returned to the Crown in exchange for a granite quarry a quarter-mile distant from the lake. Though the main lodge was salvageable, the unwinterized cabins built on slabs were beyond repair. Pat O'Connor, one of John's sons, then thirty-

Opposite: Emerald Lake Lodge, its roofline echoing the peaks above it, affords a serene view from an outdoor sitting area, a balcony, or almost any secluded spot. This page: Peace and personal reflection at the boat launch.

one, and his wife, Connie, rose to the challenge. But shortly after renovations began in 1981, the economy went into recession and interest rates skyrocketed. The other partners dropped out, and the original plans had to be scaled back. Even so, construction costs rose because new cabins had to be built on steel piles driven into the glacial rock. Pat recalls how a family tradition of perseverance carried him through; he says all was for the best. The granite quarry became the new site of new water and sewage systems and provided out-of-view parking for automobiles. Because plans were scaled down, Pat says, "We ended up with a development that was less capital-intensive and more in keeping with the environment. The historic lodge remains by far the biggest building on the site. That's the way it should be." In the process, Pat and Connie's careers took a turn: They now also own Buffalo Mountain Lodge and Deer Lodge, as well as several award-winning restaurants nearby.

Emerald Lake Lodge reopened in 1986 with eighty-five guest rooms in twenty-four chalet-style buildings. The O'Connors restored, renovated, and expanded the historic 1902 lodge. The chalets have stone fireplaces for which wood is delivered daily, rustic furnishings and feather duvets; their balconies overlook the lake. There's a clubhouse with an outdoor hot tub, dry sauna, and exercise equipment. The buildings, sited on a thirteen-acre peninsula on the lake, are the only

ones there—4,262 feet above sea level, surrounded by the President Range and the pristine wilderness of Yoho National Park, encompassing 500 square miles on the eastern border of British Columbia.

A two-and-a-half-hour drive from Calgary International Airport, Emerald Lake Lodge is isolated and at the same time easy to get to, rustic yet refined. The lodge's Mount Burgess Dining Room was one of the pioneers in the new Rocky Mountain cuisine. It emphasizes organically raised elk, bison, and caribou, raised on an O'Connor family farm dating to 1932, one of the oldest in Alberta. The lodge's Kicking Horse Bar is an authentic 1890 import from the Yukon; it and the dining room are known for their boutique wines. Just beyond the threshold of each guest cabin are miles of hiking trails, fishing, and cross-country skiing, and there's a daily shuttle to Lake Louise during ski season.

What isn't at Emerald Lake Lodge is as important as what is. Cell phones don't work. Guest rooms have no TVs, and, though the game room does have a TV, people often find the library, billiard table, and piano more alluring. There are no water slides, concession stands, crowds, noise, or bright lights, unless it is the creaking of the pines in the wind, or the full moon's reflection on fresh-fallen snow.

This page and opposite: Stone and wood distinguish Emerald Lake's interiors, whether in a chalet guest room or suite, casual eatery or formal dining room, where massive interior beams and a stunning bay window enhance a gourmet experience.

Flathead Lake Lodge

1. The Cowboy must never shoot first, hit a smaller man, or take unfair advantage. 2. He must never go back on his word, or a trust confided in him. 3. He must always tell the truth. 4. He must be gentle with children, the elderly, and animals. 5. He must not advocate or possess racially or religiously intolerant ideas. 6. He must help people in distress. 7. He must be a good worker. 8. He must keep himself clean in thought, speech, action, and personal habits. 9. He must respect women, parents, and his nation's laws. 10. The Cowboy is a patriot.
—Gene Autry's Cowboy Code

THE BEST OF THE WEST ON A FAMILY DUDE RANCH IN MONTANA

Flathead Lake Lodge, a 2,000-acre family-operated mountain dude ranch on the shore of the largest freshwater lake in the West, is a place where a kid might grow up to be the kind of person that actor Gene Autry idealized. Built in 1932 as a boys' camp, it was acquired by Les Averill, a World War II veteran who returned to Montana in 1945 to realize his own boyhood dream. Averill had always wanted to operate a dude ranch and hunting lodge where people—city folk—could experience the West. In 1971, one of his eight sons, Doug Averill, took the reins from his father; Doug and his family still live at the ranch.

Located near Bigfork, Montana, just fifteen miles south of Kalispell, not far from Glacier National Park, Flathead Lake Lodge feels remote but is easy to get to from Glacier National Park Airport, by ranch shuttle from the Amtrak station in Whitefish, by private plane, or by car. Over the years the ranch has attracted celebrities and dignitaries, but the Averills are prouder of the fact that more than 70 percent of their guests return year after year. Many are second- and third-generation guests who want their children and grandchildren to share an experience they themselves

had as kids. Maintaining its own idea of what makes a memorable family vacation—Western hospitality combined with spectacular recreational opportunities people can enjoy at their own pace—Flathead Lake Lodge has been an enduring success.

The lake, measuring thirty miles by fifteen miles at its widest points, is named after the Flathead, or Salish, Indians. The tribe welcomed Lewis and Clark to their lodges in 1804, and were painted by George Catlin between 1830 and 1836. Aided by Clark, who had become Missouri territorial governor and superintendent of Indian affairs, Catlin made five trips and visited fifty tribes, then toured an exhibit of paintings and artifacts to cities in the United States and Europe.

Native Americans, including the Flathead, also created their own art. Beginning in about 1600, the Plains Indians made biographic images depicting battle exploits and bravery, etched into the West's abundant sandstone or painted on cliffs. Later, they painted pictures on buffalo hides and tepees. In 1834, with Catlin's encouragement, Mandan warriors put their art on paper. Thus began a rare art form: Indian art done in ledger books, containing white paper usually ruled with blue lines, that were used to keep accounts. These became more common after 1860, and Indian prisoners were often given these books, along with colored pencils, to create art that was sold, or kept for its own sake. The second-known ledger book dates from 1842, when Flathead chief Five Crows created pictographs showing battles between his tribe and the Blackfeet. American Jesuit Pierre Jean De Smet, missionary to the tribe from 1841 to 1847, annotated the pictures, based upon Five Crows' explanations of the drawings. The Five Crows ledger languished in a Jesuit archive for more than 150 years before being rediscovered and published by scholar Dr. James Keyser in the 1990s. The Flathead tribe lives south of the lake, on land it shares with the Kootenai.

Legends of the West wouldn't be complete without both Indians and cowboys. From the early twentieth century, Glacier National Park activities and publicity promoted the cowboy and horse as symbols of freedom, solid values, and adventure—as did the era's

Flathead Lake Lodge
P.O. Box 248
Bigfork, MT 59911
406-837-4391
www.flatheadlakelodge.com

popular literature, traveling Wild West shows, and dude ranches. Though the high, glaciered mountains of northern Montana never figured large in the range-cattle business, cowboy guides have been leading tenderfeet on horseback into the high country and entertaining them around campfires for a century. And dudes, male and female, young and not, have donned hats, chaps, boots, and spurs, learning to ride and rope with the best of 'em.

Here at Flathead Lake, guests do all of that and more. Everyone can ride every day. Guided by one of the lodge's experienced wranglers, even little bucka-

roos, age six years and older, take "their own horses" on mountain trails. Junior wranglers learn about saddling, grooming, and barn duties, and pardner up with the cowboys and cowgirls to learn how to care for a large herd of horses. There are riding lessons, rodeos, team roping, games on horseback, pancake breakfast rides, and teen and adult rides to the nearby mountains, along the lake, and in the ranch's private game reserve with elk and buffalo. There's even a horseback ride to an old-fashioned steak fry, complete with campfire, vintage chuck wagon, and live music, like the songs Gene Autry sang. Like other meals at the ranch, the dinner barbecue features wholesome food including fresh-baked bread, and is served family-style. At this ranch, everyone is on a first-name basis.

There is terrific sailing, boating, and fishing. The ranch's fleet of sailboats include a fourteen-foot

This page: Flathead Lake's horses know to mind the cowgirls. Opposite: Ridin' and ropin' in one of the Ranch's rodeos; jumping off the dock; and sailing circa-1928, fifty-one-foot racing sloops, prototypes for America's Cup boats.

Vagabond and two twenty-seven-foot Olympic Solings, as well as more advanced boats that novices can learn to sail with help of the ranch's waterfront wranglers. Best of all, guests can go for a sail, crewed by the ranch's staff, aboard two historic fifty-one-foot Q-class racing sloops, the Questa and the Nor'Easter, built in 1928 and 1929 as prototypes for America's Cup boats. It's hard to decide which is better, to watch the majestic boats from the saddle or the magnificent horses from on deck, so most people choose both. Kayakers and canoers can take off for a quiet paddle; anglers can elect to don waders, go fly-fishing, or borrow a boat for lake fishing; waterskiers and Boogie Boarders can churn up some wake. Several times a week, sightseeing cruises take guests around the lake and up the Flathead River through a water fowl preserve to view osprey and bald eagles. Guests can

start the day with a game of tennis, get up a volleyball game, or play one-on-one basketball on the ranch's courts; equipment is available in the recreation room. Just a few miles away is golf at the twenty-seven-hole Eagle Bend Golf Course, considered Montana's best.

The ranch's stylish log buildings include historic lodges with sitting areas, lofts, and river-stone fireplaces, which can accommodate up to four people, and cabins comprising two- and three-bedroom units with porches overlooking the lake. Log furnishings, Western accents, handmade quilts, calico fabrics, and bouquets of wildflowers add up to a homey, stylish ambience.

After a full day at Flathead Lake, dudes and cowboys gather at happy hour in the ranch's Saddle Sore Saloon. Or they might relax around a fire, stretch out on a buffalo-hide couch, or absorb the beautiful lake view. By the time they retire to bed and their heads hit the pillow, all that fresh air, activity, and good food will have done its work. People sleep soundly here, and when they dream of cowboys, it's a sign that Averill's Flathead Lake Lodge has branded another city slicker for life.

This page: After a day in the saddle, a cozy room with homey quilts and log beds spells comfort. Opposite: Before dinner, wranglers—their jeans well broken in by now—mingle in front of the Ranch's massive stone fireplace.

The Hermosa Inn

What's inside of a lariat loop? A steer's head, yes, or a snorting stallion. But symbolically it takes [in] even more than that. If the cowboy has imagination, the loop of his yearning takes in all he sees and knows and loves, and if he has friendliness, he wants most of all to share those things.
—Oren Arnold, Portfolio, *Cowboy Builds a Loop*, 1944

A COWBOY ARTIST'S STUDIO
IN THE SONORAN DESERT

The Western frontier has always been the place where Americans have gone to reinvent themselves. One of them was Lon Megargee, a Philadelphia boy who lit out for the territories, changed his name, learned to rope and ride, became an artist, claimed the new state of Arizona as his birthplace, and was reborn in the mythic image of the cowboy.

In 1934, Megargee bought a speck of Arizona desert with dramatic views of Camelback Mountain. In 1935, during the depths of the Great Depression, "gambling his last dollar" on the place, he began construction of an artist's studio/residence. He made rough sketches to aid the process, then relied on instinct, spontaneity, and craft to build it. Inspired by regional architecture he had seen in Spain, Mexico, and New Mexico, he designed a one-room residence with a mission-style tower as his art studio. He built the house by hand, using wood timbers and adobe blocks made on site. When he was done, he painted a Mexican caballero on the exterior of the tower.

Casa Hermosa, or "beautiful home," as it came to be called, was one of six houses Megargee is known to have designed and built; several still stand in Phoenix, Cave Creek, and Sedona. Megargee's interest in regionalism, historical appropriateness, and Southwestern building techniques and materials was a precursor of the Santa Fe style.

As Megargee had time and money, he expanded the house. To earn income, he added two small

Opposite: At this one-time artist's retreat, savoring a good meal as the sunset colors the sky, guests are reminded that living life to the fullest may be the greatest art of all.

guest houses, each consisting of a living room with a corner fireplace and a bedroom, which he rented. Megargee lived and worked at Casa Hermosa until 1941, when he sold it. Several owners and additions later, the hacienda was converted into a guest ranch, and eventually an inn. Subsequent owners added a swimming pool, tennis courts, casitas, and villas.

In 1987, a fire damaged the main building, Megargee's original home. Attracted by the property's past and promise, Paradise Valley residents Fred and Jennifer Unger bought the hotel in 1992 and led a restoration project to reclaim the original charm and tradition of the historic structure.

Sited on six acres of lush desert in residential Paradise Valley between Phoenix and Scottsdale, the Hermosa was painstakingly restored to give guests an authentic sense of Arizona's Wild West era. Today, the inn is both a historic landmark and an elegant retreat, combining the feeling of a country inn with the amenities of a first-class resort. Adobe walls, wooden beams and vaulted ceilings, mesquite wood doors, reclaimed brick, rustic floor tiles, and hand-painted Mexican tiles flow seamlessly through the public spaces, meeting rooms, and restaurant, which has won awards for its healthful, organically oriented gourmet American cuisine. These features, along with the hotel's stone and beehive fireplaces, over-size hand-carved furniture, and vintage Western artifacts create a timeless, rustic-yet-refined ambience.

In the library, for instance, are a massive stone fireplace, vintage leather and wood period furniture, many pieces of Megargee's artwork, and walls of bookcases showcasing a collection of more than 450 antique books. One bookcase wall folds back, completely opening the room to an adjoining meeting room.

The Hermosa's thirty-five guest rooms—no two alike—comprise casitas, suites, and freestanding two-bedroom villas. Private patios, courtyards, gardens with sunken spas, mesquite trees and flowering oleander, and an abundance of artistic details add to their charm. High-speed Internet service assures that even seclusion need not mean isolation.

The Hermosa Inn
5532 North Palo Cristi Road
Scottsdale, AZ 85253
800-241-1210
www.hermosainn.com

Megargee's art, including original paintings, lithographs, pencil sketches, and posters, is on display throughout the hotel. The Grand Canyon and other natural wonders, lounging cowboys, adobe pueblos, chiefs in feather war bonnets, men on horseback, Spanish padres, cattle drives, Indian drummers and dances, beautiful women, and wizened prospectors populate his work. Soft-hued or jolted with bright color, Megargee's oil paintings present a mythic, colorful, romanticized image of the West.

The artist himself was as colorful and mythic as his paintings. Born in Philadelphia in 1883, with the surname "Megarge," the boy devoured the pulp Western novels of the day. After a visit to Buffalo Bill Cody's Wild West Show, he hopped a westbound train, arrived in Phoenix in 1896, milked cows and mended fences, and worked as a policeman, fireman, and stud poker dealer before taking a job as a ranch hand and becoming an exhibition roper with Arizona Charlie's Wild West Show. It was a step down from Buffalo Bill, but one in the right direction. He moved from ranch to ranch, honing his skills as a cowboy, adding an "e" to his name to affiliate with a Philadelphia family more prominent than his own. By 1906, he was half-owner of a ranch; three years later, ruined by drought, he gave it up.

"If I had prospered as a rancher, chances are I'd . . . never have put paint to canvas," he said.

Megargee had always sketched on the ranch, and he studied art in Los Angeles and his hometown, yet at various times, he claimed to have had no art training and to have trained at art schools more renowned than those he did attend. Whether to advance his career or because he saw himself this way, he revised his personal history, reinventing himself as the mythic cowboy. He perfected his swagger, claimed to be an Arizona native, made sure he was frequently photographed—slouching on a horse, eyes narrowed under the Stetson's brim.

Megargee drank, joked, and partied hard, parlaying his good looks and rugged charisma into at least six marriages and a longer string of broken hearts. Raucous, rowdy, and reliable as a tumbleweed, he let

This page and opposite: The Hermosa Inn offers varied places for gourmet dining and entertaining: in its main dining room, boardroom, and wine cellar, where Lon Megargee's paintings recall the life of this Western artist.

money slip through his fingers like so much desert sand, but he was, after all, a cowboy—a bit larger than life. About himself and about the West, he was an unrepentant idealist.

"Out here on the desert one is able to concentrate away from the turmoil of life. . . one lives in a more wholesome, saner way," Megargee wrote in a letter to Arizona's first governor, George Hunt. ". . . seeing the sun rise out of the desert in the morning—a glimpse of distant mountains that always spell great promise to me. The whole expanse of nature as I see her inspires in me the desire to strive for the highest attainment possible—with my work, thoughts, and actual living."

In 1912, shortly after Arizona attained statehood, Megargee was commissioned to paint fifteen large canvases for the State Capitol. In his first brush with fame, he created murals depicting Arizona themes: the Grand Canyon and other natural wonders, Native American life, Spanish colonial settlement, agriculture, ranching, and mining. Other important commissions came from the Santa Fe Railroad, and Governor Hunt owned the largest private collection of his work. Megargee's few commercial art projects included creating the famous "last drop" image on the inside of all Stetson hats. You'll see some of those vintage Stetsons, along with lariats, at the Hermosa Inn.

This page: Guest rooms, suites, and villas like this one with a private patio are decorated with hefty wooden and upholstered pieces, iron bedsteads, and Western accessories in varied colors and textures to delight the eye.

High Wild & Lonesome

I want to ride to the ridge where the West commences,
and gaze at the moon 'til I lose my senses.
I can't look at hovels and I can't stand fences.
Don't fence me in.
—Cole Porter and Robert H. Fletcher

EARNING YOUR SPURS IN WYOMING'S HIGH DESERT

The fire, a short distance from the camp wagon, flickers in the dimming light and sends a ribbon of smoke into the cooling air. Nearby, the cattle are grazing by the willows bordering the creek, and farther out, on the fragrant sage. Deer, antelope, and gray sage hens venture out of the aspen grove and down to the stream for water. As the tired riders walk to their tents, there is only the lowing of the cattle, the bawling of the calves, the sea of stars in the vast blue-black sky, and from far off the howl of a coyote.

High Wild & Lonesome is a destination without a building. Bobbie and Mike Wade, the outfitters who own and operate the company, were raised on family ranches in eastern Wyoming, not far from the Pony Express Trail and the Texas Cattle Trail. Both their fathers worked as cowboys before buying their own spreads. Bobbie and Mike started working their families' herds from about the age of five, trailing and branding cattle, training colts, mending fences, haying, irrigating, and taking feed out to the herds in the winter. They've worked as ranch hands, big-game hunting guides, wranglers, mule packers, and cooks. They have been outfitters for more than thirty-five years and have spent more hours in the saddle than they can count. Their aim with High Wild & Lonesome is to share the legacy of their cowboy upbringing and give guests an accurate understanding of that lifestyle.

What the Wades do is take a few people each week out to the open range to sleep in tepees under the stars, eat wholesome dinners cooked over an open campfire,

Opposite: Beauty in simplicity, a concept often cited but rarely lived, is here in Wyoming, where a tepee and the star-strewn night sky are accommodation enough after visiting the protected mustang herds that run wild and free.

lope across the desert to see wild mustangs, or herd cattle, from 500 to 1,500 head of them, depending upon the day. This experience is not a nose-to-tail trail ride; it's trotting and cantering on seasoned quarter horses. Most rides cover upward of fifteen to twenty-five miles a day, and cattle drives mean early mornings and long hours in the saddle. The Wades only take six people out each week, including teens over the age of sixteen. Riders under the age of twenty-one must be accompanied by a parent or guardian, and beginners need not apply.

The nearest major airports to High Wild & Lonesome's departure point are in Salt Lake City, about 180 miles away by shuttle service, and Jackson, Wyoming, which is about 90 miles by car. Once guests settle in at the campsite, the riding begins. In an orientation Bobbie describes as "Horseback 101," the Wades review horse psychology, behavior and safety, saddling, bridling, and the proper way to mount and dismount. Then guests mount up and show their stuff. High Wild & Lonesome offers fifteen weeklong riding itineraries each year from June through October.

One of them is the Roundup & Cattle Drive, conducted in early summer and in the fall. In June, riders move cattle across the fresh spring range to the high-country summer pastures, and in October, they gather the herd and move them back to winter in the valleys. These are working cattle drives, the kind that originated after the end of the Civil War when Texas cattlemen returned home to find their herds had increased in number to an estimated six million, mostly longhorns. The person who first made the link between all those steers and the demand for beef in Eastern cities was Illinois meatpacker Joseph G. McCoy, who convinced the Kansas Pacific Railroad to run stock cars from Abilene, Kansas. In 1867, the great trail drives began. Cowboys rounded up Texas longhorns into herds and drove them to the open-range country of the northern plains to fatten them up before shipping them from western towns like Cheyenne, Wyoming. Some thirty years later, barbed-wire fences crisscrossed the prairie, the refrigerated railway car had been invented, and railroad expansion made the great drives unnecessary. But by then they had given birth to the American cowboy.

High Wild & Lonesome
P.O. Box 116
Big Piney, WY 83113
877-276-3485
www.hwl.net

Civil War veterans, African Americans, Mexicans, Native Americans, and women all worked as cowboys. Slaves, experienced in tending herds in Africa, were often given that job in the American South; African-American Willie M. Pickett, born in 1870 near Austin, Texas, is credited with the invention of steer wrestling, or "bulldogging," as it was originally known. As early as the 1830s, Sally Skull (her second husband's surname) took over her father's ranch and was riding, roping, and branding cattle with her own mark on the Texas frontier; given to wearing rawhide bloomers, she killed a man with her six-gun, fought Indians, and traded horses across the Mexican border. Between 1886 and 1889, Lizzie Johnson, known as the "Queen of the Trail Drivers," was the first woman to drive her herd over the Chisholm Trail.

Competence, persistence, pride, courage, and loyalty are still the qualities that rule this meritocracy, and, with High Wild & Lonesome, the cattle drive is one place to test them, riding stirrup to stirrup with working cowboys.

One of the unusual features about High Wild & Lonesome is the opportunity to ride in the Red Desert and view wild mustangs. Several itineraries, called Wild Horse Heaven, are devoted to that. The bloodline of the wild mustang traces to sixteen Spanish barb horses brought by Cortez to the Americas. Prized for their speed and agility, mustangs were used by the U.S.

This page: Wild mustang, a tent, and an American flag, all at home in the Red Desert. Opposite: High Wild & Lonesome's riding itineraries include cattle drives in June and October, and moments of mutual appreciation shared by horse and rider.

Cavalry, the Texas Rangers, and the Pony Express; many were driven north with the cattle to be sold to ranches where they were crossed with Morgans and other breeds. In 1971, Congress passed legislation protecting the " . . . wild free-roaming horses . . . [that] are fast disappearing. . . . "

The wild horses have a perfect home in the 2.5-million-acre Great Divide Basin, a remote territory of sage, sand, bunch grass, hidden water holes, and wide open spaces. Protected by mountains on three sides, the Great Divide Basin is the only place where the Continental Divide splits and rejoins, creating a basin where the water remains rather than flowing to the Atlantic or Pacific. It is part of the eight-million-acre Red Desert, also known as the Great American Desert, which encompasses the largest active sand dune system in North America. It is home to the nation's largest desert elk herd and migratory game herd (pronghorn antelope), and more than 350 wildlife species.

It's a great place to ride, a country of mountain peaks and red-rimmed canyons, crystal mountain streams and the clear waters of the Green and Sweetwater Rivers, and more than four million acres of public land with hundred-mile views between horizons. There are old Pony Express stations along the way. Not too far distant is the Green River Rendezvous, a meeting point for trappers and mountain men like Jim Bridger, whose name figures large in this part of Wyoming. There's also South Pass, the twenty-mile-wide valley across the Continental Divide, the only such passage through the Rockies, used by pioneer wagon trains on the Oregon Trail. Between 1843 and 1912, 400,000 settlers crossed South Pass. For many pioneers, this was the point

where the West commenced. Fences are still few and far between.

The concept of natural horsemanship, which emphasizes teamwork between horse and rider, is prominent in all of High Wild & Lonesome's programs. Two week-long Two as One™ clinics are held in the wide open spaces, and provide coaching and time with the wild mustangs. Among the things riders learn is what the Wades promise is the "one control technique that works every time." The high point of this week is a night ride in the high desert. Horses, it seems, see very well in the dark.

For novice riders and people looking for a quieter horseback vacation, two relaxed Fall Color rides take guests through groves of yellow, gold, and orange-leafed cottonwood and aspen. High Wild & Lonesome also offers vacations exclusively for women. Aptly called Cowgirl Up!, these can be scheduled on any of its itineraries. (In 1869, when it was still a territory, Wyoming was the first place in the United States to give women the right to vote.)

The life of the cowboy hasn't changed much in the last hundred years, except for the amenities on the trail. Even though High Wild & Lonesome's guests are "roughing it"—often saddling their horses before sunup, braving all kinds of temperatures and weather, and wearing some dust—when they ride into camp at the end of the day, there are hot showers, comfortable foam pads under the sleeping bags, camp "easy chairs," a civilized portable toilet, and pre-dinner hors d'oeuvres and cocktails, the latter on a bring-your-own basis. It is amazing what a good camp cook can accomplish over an open fire: grilled steak, chili, "cowboy coffee," breads, biscuits and desserts baked in a Dutch oven, and lots of salads and produce, something that was sorely lacking in the "grub" served to nineteenth-century cowboys.

Out here, city slickers might feel they've learned something about the West, and that it's not just about riding and roping. In the heart of the high desert, hidden away in the most temporary of shelters, right before a person drifts off to sleep, there is the scent of wood smoke from the campfire, the memory of a wild mustang, and a more elemental truth: As John Muir once said, "We all live in one room—the world with the firmament for its roof—and are sailing the celestial spaces without leaving any track."

Opposite: It's amazing what a good camp cook can accomplish over an open fire—"cowboy coffee," biscuits baked in a Dutch oven, and steaks. This page: Mike Wade sits his quarter horse like he was born in the saddle.

Hogan Under the Stars

I have been to the end of the earth.
I have been to the end of the waters.
I have been to the end of the sky.
I have been to the end of the mountains.
I have found none that are not my friends.
—DinÂ (Navajo) proverb

LIFE ON THE RESERVATION

Navajo Nation sprawls across the Southwest, extending into Utah, Arizona, and New Mexico. It is the largest Indian reservation in the United States. Established in 1868 after the Navajo were released from their imprisonment at the Bosque Redondo, it covers more than fifteen million acres and contains over 9,000 miles of paved roads. It encompasses desert, mountains, canyons and arroyos, lakes, ancient Anasazi ruins, Chaco Canyon, Monument Valley, the Chuska and Lukachukai mountain ranges, Little Colorado River Gorge, Canyon de Chelly, Window Rock, Antelope Canyon, Ship Rock (the eroded volcanic core sacred to the Navajo that rises 1,700 feet into the air), and Hubbell's Trading Post (the oldest continuously operating store in the country) located in Ganado, Arizona. More than 168,000 DinÂ, as the Navajo call themselves, live on the reservation, in homes clustered around chapter houses and widely scattered in more remote areas. For travelers who want to escape the myth of the American Indian and experience the real thing, the Hogan Under the Stars, thirty miles from Ganado, is a good place to start.

Guests won't find electric lines in this part of the reservation; the Hogan and the nearby home of its owners run on solar power and a converter. They won't find indoor plumbing here, either. The Hogan Under the Stars has an old-fashioned wash basin, kerosene lamps, and a wood stove. Once a week, David Abe, who built the Hogan and lives next door, drives his pickup truck, which is equipped with a 200-gallon water tank, to a well about ten miles away, fills the tank, drives home,

and fills a storage tank on the property. The Hogan has an outhouse, and the chapter house in Cornfields, six miles away, has showers. On much of the reservation, there is no mail delivery, no trash collection, no telephone or cellular service. Unemployment is at 50 percent.

It might seem strange that a boy raised in Barstow and Los Angeles would choose this way of life. David Abe did, because his heritage meant more to him than all the modern amenities California had to offer. Orphaned early in life, Abe left the reservation at the age of five to live with an uncle. When he returned to visit relatives, it always felt like coming home. He moved to the Navajo Nation at the age of fourteen, returned to Los Angeles to finish high school, worked in California, and finally returned to Arizona in 1996. Shortly thereafter, at the Ganado medical clinic, he met his wife, Kathleen, an Anglo nurse from Ohio. After getting out of the Army, she answered an ad in a nursing journal to work on the reservation. The Abes' five children are all homeschooled.

What David and Kathleen appreciate about the reservation is what few tourists ever get to experience fully. Life here has a slower rhythm. Conversations are less chatty, more punctuated with thoughtful silences. There's a strong connection to the earth and a sensitivity to one's place in it. There is the deep ancestral understanding that gives substance to dances and songs, and meaning to the patterns of a rug or blanket, jar, or basket. When David Abe returned to live on the reservation, these are the kinds of things he was seeking. The reason he built the Hogan Under the Stars was to share his heritage, and the real experience of living on the reservation, with his guests.

The traditional hogan the Navajo have been building since at least 1680 is a round one-room structure with no windows and a doorway facing east. Its exterior form is modeled after two of the DinÂ's sacred mountains—the fine, tapering shape of Gobernador Knob, and the rounded top of Huerfano Mesa, where legend says the first hogan was built. The hogan fit the terrain, partly because of its materials, partly because it was an expression of the Native Americans' concept that

Hogan Under the Stars
P.O. Box 1287
Ganado, AZ 86505
928-755-3273

Opposite: The door of Hogan Under the Stars in Arizona, in the Navajo Nation. Its owners live next door. Black-and-white photo: Historic Navajo hogan in Ganado, Arizona, circa 1900.

A NAVAJO INDIAN HOGAN,
GANADO, ARIZONA.
GANADO MISSION GIFT

they are simply part of the earth, like the soil, grasses, wildflowers, or buffalo. "The American Indian," Luther Standing Bear, an Oglala Sioux, wrote, "fits into the landscape, for the hand that fashioned the continent also fashioned the man for his surroundings." The hogan's interior embraces those within it, linking them with the earth and sky. Traditionally, a hole in the center of its roof allowed sunlight to enter, air to flow, smoke from a central fire to rise, and a view of the sky. Floors were always made of dirt, because the Diné consider the earth strengthening and healing, and being closer to it is a way to be closer to life's meaning and to others. More than a building, the hogan is a symbol of the Navajos' place in the world. In the hogan, women sit on the north, men on the south, and visitors on the west, the place of honor because it faces the door and the sunrise. Upon entering for a ceremony, everyone moves clockwise, as the sun does in its arc across the sky.

Most important, the hogan is sacred space. Whether its intended use is ceremonial or residential, it is blessed by anointing its four major beams with cornmeal or pollen before it is used. Blessings are done before major ceremonies or if a family has been away a long time.

The Navajo Blessingway, a spiritual ceremony, describes the first hogan in poetic and mythic terms as a "House made of dawn, House made of evening twilight, House made of dark cloud, House made of male rain, House made of dark mist, House made of female rain, House made of pollen, House made of grasshoppers. . . ." The chant ties the hogan to the creation of Diné culture and contains construction specifications. Legend says that Coyote, a significant figure to many Native American tribes, suggested that First Man and First Woman build a hogan of cottonwood logs like those of the beaver. The traditional "first hogan" is a pyramid with five triangular faces constructed on what the Navajo call a fork-stick frame. Three forked vertical logs were set in the ground at the north, west, and south points so that the forks interlocked at the top. Two straight logs were placed against these on the east side to form a doorway opening to the first light of dawn, two

An old Navajo Indian house, or Hogan, in New Mexico.

This page and opposite: Comfortable furnishings and daily necessities take on the quality of a still-life painting. Historic black-and-white photos: Light filters into the interior of a summer hogan; hogan in New Mexico; ceremonial hogan.

more over the door frame of the entrance, and a final log is placed crosswise at the top of the chimney.

There are said to be two types of hogans—male and female—depending upon structure and use. The fork-tip structure of the sort Coyote built is a male hogan used for ceremonies. The larger female hogan, twenty or more feet in diameter, houses the family. Historically, it was of cribbed-log construction: Notched logs were laid horizontally, in a prescribed manner, with the builder moving clockwise and placing root ends to the west and growing ends to the east; logs were inter-locked at the corners to form five walls. The roof, built of layers of logs, was domed. To insulate against the wind and cold, the exterior was thickly covered with packed clay, which became watertight when dry. This gave the female hogan a soft, rounded shape. Other types of hogans include sweat lodges. The Navajo began build-ing hexagonal and octagonal hogans like David Abe's in the early 1900s.

DinÂ who practice traditional religion use hogans for ceremonies, healings, and to keep themselves grounded and in balance. Though some outlying hogans are seasonal shelters for sheepherders, most today are private spiritual centers. The Hogan Under the Stars is what an architect might call a multiuse hogan. Ceremonies are held here, songs are sung, prayers are offered. But, furnished with a cozy wood stove, vintage russet velvet sofa, bureau, armoire, twin beds with handmade quilts, table, chairs, and plenty of space for sleeping bags, it is also a dwelling place that welcomes visitors.

Tourists can experience what it is like to be inside a hogan in several units built for this purpose, includ-ing one at the Navajo Nation Zoo and Botanical Park in Window Rock and one at the Monument Valley park site. In these settings there is no fear of trespassing or intruding on private property. At DinÂ College in Tsaile, Arizona, the first Indian-owned community college in the nation, the hogan is reinterpreted in the octagonal glass-walled, six-story Hatathli Museum and Gallery, a very modern building.

Visitors in the Navajo Nation will be thrilled by dances, drumming and songs, hear about tribal history, admire silver necklaces studded with turquoise, and get a sense of the vibrant culture the DinÂ maintain against high odds. Since a majority of older DinÂ speak Navajo, visitors may hear firsthand the language of the code talkers who helped win World War II.

But ordinary tourists won't have the pleasure of a home-cooked breakfast burrito wrapped in an extra-thick Navajo tortilla or an evening walk with their host to observe birds and wildlife. They won't end the day enclosed in a circle, sitting by a warming wood stove whose chimney reaches through the center of the roof. Hidden away in the Hogan Under the Stars, the traveler can learn what it is to walk in another man's moccasins.

This page and opposite: Furnishings, including fluffy towels and a vintage wash basin, encircle a wood-burning stove. Its chimney reaches through a hole in the fork-beamed roof—traditional features of hogan construction. Historic black-and-white photo: This hogan takes its shape from Gobernador Knob.

The Inn of the Five Graces

When [the Santa Fe Trail] was established across the great plains as a line of communication to the shores of the blue Pacific...travel was by the slow freight caravan drawn by patient oxen, or the lumbering stage coach with its complement of four to six mules.
—W.F. Cody, "Buffalo Bill"

THE SANTA FE TRAIL MEETS THE SILK ROAD IN NEW MEXICO

Beginning in 1565, Spanish galleons, laden with Asian ceramics, textiles, and furnishings, crossed the Pacific from Manila to Mexico. The galleons were called "nao de la Chine" or "the ships of China." In Mexico, their exotic cargo was loaded onto mule trains headed either for the Caribbean where waiting ships would carry it to Spain, or for the dusty trails of the Camino Real—the Spanish King's Highway of the Interior Lands—into New Mexico, Texas, and California. The galleon trade continued for 250 years, until 1815.

Despite technologies that make the world seem smaller every day, the furnishings in the Inn of the Five Graces came by similar means, in containers on modern merchant ships from central and east Asia all the way to Santa Fe, a reminder that the city has long been a crossroads of diverse cultural influences—including Native American, Spanish, Anglo, and Asian.

The Inn of the Five Graces encompasses all of these. Located just a block from the old Santa Fe Trail, it stands next to the oldest church in the nation, the San Miguel Mission, and Santa Fe's oldest residence—the settlement on the "other side of the water," the south side of the Santa Fe River—in the Barrio de Analco. One of Santa Fe's oldest neighborhoods, this is where the Spanish housed the Tlaxcalan Indians, whom they brought to Santa Fe to become their servants after the Tlaxcalan helped Cortez defeat Montezuma and the Aztecs. The Spanish lived on the north side of the river.

Opposite: The Inn of the Five Graces' patio in Santa Fe is a colorful, yet restful setting to dine alfresco or loll on a lounge chair, while the balcony above offers a shady spot to relax.

The inn's name derives from a Tibetan custom of presenting five gifts to a holy lama before embarking on a journey. Each gift is given to secure a blessing for the trip to come, and each represents one of the five graces—the five senses through which we experience the world: sight, sound, smell, touch, and taste. In 2003, nine visiting Tibetan monks, clad in saffron robes and headdresses and chanting as they walked slowly through the labyrinth of rooms, bestowed ancient Buddhist blessings of peace, prosperity, and good health on the inn and its guests.

An intimate enclave of historic structures, the Inn of the Five Graces consists of a long, one-story adobe building, a two-story 1938 stone house built of rocks taken from the Santa Fe River, a maze of courtyards leading to terraces and gardens complete with fountains, Buddhist and Hindu statuary, Japanese elms and flowering plants, and twenty uniquely appointed suites. The suites comprise living rooms, bedrooms, and private baths, as relaxed and reclusive as a private home. This home away from home, however, is an amazing alchemy of color and texture—honey-hued adobe walls, carved wooden bedsteads and columns from Tibet, silk pillows and hangings, hand-painted beams, thatched straw ceilings, sofas upholstered with Turkish kilims, stone and tile floors spread with Afghan carpets, and a sumptuous mix of Hindu, Buddhist, Islamic, and Native American furnishings and art.

The inn's original furnishings were selected by Ira and Sylvia Seret, who created the bed-and-breakfast in the mid-1990s. Sylvia designed many of the colorful tile and mosaic patterns in the inn's kitchens and baths. A showcase for the imported furniture and textiles from the couple's Santa Fe store, Seret & Sons, the Inn of the Five Graces quickly absorbed a quantity of handcrafted wooden screens, doors, mirrors, kilims, and chests from Tibet, Afghanistan, and India.

Several years later, David and Christie Garrett, of the Garrett Hotel Group, visited the inn as guests. On impulse they made an offer, and the inn soon joined their select group of singular hotels. The Garrett Group undertook some renovations, added two guest

The Inn of the Five Graces
150 E. DeVargas Street
Santa Fe, NM 87501
505-992-0957
www.fivegraces.com

rooms, and created a welcoming area for guests, complete with a library, breakfast area, and billiard table. They brought in furnishings compatible with the Serets' choices, along with the company's signature feather beds. A landscape designer with an interest in theatrical set design, Christie's focus has been to make each of the Inn of the Five Graces' garden courtyards and guest suites an experience to please the senses.

The staff goes to some lengths to do this. Service begins even before one's arrival, with a call to ask about favorite culinary treats for the guest room larder, a supply the staff will replenish throughout one's stay. Seasonal lodging packages geared to the five senses theme include photography workshops, cooking classes, concerts by performers with the Santa Fe Opera, and hands-on workshops with local artists and artisans.

Though in the center of town, the Inn of the Five Graces is close to outdoor activities, including horseback riding, hot-air ballooning, and hiking. It is little more than a chip shot away from Santa Fe's finest golf courses. Black Mesa Golf Club, designed by Baxter Spann and considered one of the best in New Mexico, is a thirty-minute drive; Towa Golf Resort, designed

Opposite: Stone walls, wood-framed windows, an Indonesian bench, and *ikat* textiles imbue candlelight dinners with a special mystique. This page: With their richly colored Asian fabrics, painted kiva fireplaces, and architectural details, guest rooms are sumptuous and exotic.

by Hale Irwin and William Phillips, with the state's only tee shot to an island green, is a twenty-minute drive; and Pueblo de Cochiti, ranked one of America's most affordable golf courses, is a forty-minute drive away. Since Santa Fe has more art galleries per square foot than any other city in the nation, and since Santa Fe Plaza and myriad shops and fine restaurants are within walking distance of the inn, golf widows and widowers might encourage their significant others to play an extra nine holes.

When guests return to their rooms, they find a Native American dream catcher on their pillows. Made of leather, wire, bright wooden beads, and feathers, the dream catcher's design derives from the colorful plumage male birds use to attract their mates: Good dreams, attracted by the colorful beads and feathers,

pass through the center circle, while bad dreams are caught in the wire web and held there until the morning sun destroys them.

At the Inn of the Five Graces, the morning sun has help: The colorful, richly appointed interiors, the tranquil silences, the scent of desert sage, and the feel of luxurious silks and cottons are gifts for the senses, assuring sweet dreams and blessings for the day to come.

This page: Bathrooms with tile mosaics and patterned textiles invite a long soak in the tub after exploring Santa Fe's art galleries. Opposite: A private breakfast outside a guest room is the perfect way to greet a new day.

Kokopelli's Cave B&B

When our earth mother is replete with living waters, when spring comes, the source of our flesh, all the different kinds of corn, we shall lay to rest in the ground. With their earth mother's living waters, the seeds will be made into new beings. Coming out standing into the daylight of their sun father, calling for rain, to all sides they will stretch out their hands.

Then, from wherever the rain makers stay, they will send forth their misty breath. Their massed clouds...will come and sit with us. . . . The clay-lined hollows of our earth mother will overflow with water. Desiring that it should be thus, I send forth my prayer.
—Zuni Prayer for Rain

AN UNDERGROUND EXPERIENCE IN THE LAND OF THE ANASAZI

In what feels like a remote location (but really just two miles north of Farmington, New Mexico), its entrance barely visible seventy feet down the vertical face of a west-facing cliff, this 1,700-square-foot cavity cutting through rock strata dating to the days of the dinosaurs is a retreat in both place and time. Kokopelli's Cave is an extreme hideaway.

The Ojo Alamo sandstone forming the cliffs where the cave is located is about sixty-five million years old, and the base of the cave is at the probable boundary between the Tertiary and Cretaceous layers of stratified rock laid down in prehistoric times. Archaeologists have found dinosaur fossils below the Ojo Alamo in the late Cretaceous Kirtland formation, which is about ninety million years old. Petrified wood, fossil wood, carbonaceous material, leaf and wood fragments, and casts, along with minor coal fragments are common in the Ojo Alamo.

If Kokopelli's Cave seems to be a geologist's dream come true, it is. Originally conceived by owners Bruce and Margie Black as an office for Black's geologic consulting, it evolved over time into a guest house,

Opposite: Cut into sandstone cliffs outside Farmington, New Mexico, its entrance barely visible in the rock, Kokopelli's Cave is a geologist's creation named for the mythical being sacred to the Zuni and other Native American tribes of the Southwest.

then into a unique bed-and-breakfast. Cozy rather than claustrophobic, it has a broad glass door in the bedroom opening to clear vistas to the west, as well as more cavelike features. The walls, especially the central column that separates the rooms, contain visible evidence of the river that once coursed here—a 360-degree view of cross bedding, petrified and carbonized wood and plant fragments, and other river-current direction indicators deposited in prehistoric stream channels. And the bathroom shower is a waterfall that cascades off a wall made of local stone set with wooden *vigas,* and can be used to fill the hot tub.

At the entrance is a flagstone-paved room leading to the living areas. There, a large central pillar separates the circular open area into separate rooms with plush carpeting and stone walls. The living room has a futon couch that sleeps two, as well as a TV and VCR and a collection of movies. A den with flagstone flooring features a stone kiva and *horno* fireplace. Adjacent to the den is a full-service kitchen and dining area. A handmade wooden queen-size bedstead decorates the bedroom. From there, a double-wide sliding glass door opens to a balcony overlooking the Plata River Valley 250 feet below. From this vantage point, guests have an incomparable view of desert sunsets and of the Four Corners, where New Mexico, Colorado, Arizona, and Utah meet.

Kokopelli's Cave is at the center of the great Anasazi Indian culture, one of the most ancient civilizations known to have existed on the continent. The Anasazi, who occupied this area from before A.D. 100 to about A.D. 1300, hunted game and cultivated crops like corn, beans, and squash; domesticated the turkey; and crafted pottery, baskets, and other objects. In settlements that stretched from the Grand Canyon to Toko'navi (Navajo Mountain), toward the Lukachukai Mountains near the New Mexico/Arizona border, and south to the Mogollon Rim, they constructed remarkable cliff dwellings of stone—hundred-room cities with towers and circular underground chambers called kivas—helping to make this Mesa Verde country one of the richest archaeological areas in North America.

Kokopelli's Cave B&B
3204 Crestridge Drive
Farmington, NM 87401
505-326-2461
www.bbonline.com/nm/kokopelli

What the Anasazi called themselves is not known: "Anasazi" is the word the Navajo used, and means "ancient enemy" or "ancient stranger." The Hopi, who, along with the Pueblo Indians, claim ancestry with the Anasazi, called them the "Hisatsinom," meaning "ones who came before" or "people of long ago." How and why the Anasazi civilization ended is a mystery still. Archaeologists have found evidence of a great drought in the late 1200s, but the Anasazi apparently began to move before that, to Zuni land in western New Mexico, Hopi mesas in northeastern Arizona, and adobe villages near the Rio Grande. The reasons might have been drought, climate change, soil depletion or overuse of other natural resources, or because of breakdowns or changes in their society. Whatever the reason, tens of thousands of Anasazi left their cities, never to return.

Opposite: Cozy rooms carved from rock contain a round kiva modeled on those in ancient Anasazi ruins nearby. This page: Interior walls contain petrified and carbonized wood and plant fragments from a prehistoric river that flowed here.

There are world-class Anasazi ruins, as well as Hopi, Pueblo, Zuni, Navajo, and Aztec sites, within driving distance from Kokopelli's Cave. The Anasazi Cultural Center and the Mesa Verde National Monument, with its world-famous cliff dwellings, are to the north. Chaco Canyon National Monument, the World Heritage Center, and the well-known Pueblo Bonito Ruins are to the south. Canyon de Chelly lies to the west in Arizona, and Hovenweep, with its tall, cylindrical tower kivas, is to the northwest in Utah. The Aztec National Monument and Salmon ruins are to the east.

As for the name of the cave, it comes from the Kokopelli character found painted and carved on rock walls and boulders throughout this region, one of the most intriguing and widespread images to have survived from ancient Anasazi culture. Kokopelli is a mischievous trickster, minstrel spirit of music, and symbol of fertility. His hump is often described as a bag of gifts, a sack containing the seeds of plants and flowers he scatters every spring. His songs are said to warm the earth, melt the winter snow, cause rain, and make the corn grow. He still is a sacred figure to the Hopi, Zuni, Taos, and Acoma pueblo peoples, and is known for his whimsical nature, kind deeds, and vital spirit.

This little reminder of the Anasazi, Kokopelli's dancing figure, with his back hunched and playing a flute, marks the road to the cave. If his flute playing lures you to it, it will also bring you out again into the sun.

This page and opposite: A waterfall shower can be used to fill a stone tub, the kitchen is well equipped, and the bedroom's large sliding-glass door has a spectacular view of the Plata River Valley to the west.

Korakia Pensione

I have not discovered very much, but at least I am now convinced that Tangier is a place where the past and the present exist simultaneously in proportionate degree, where a very much alive today is given an added depth of reality by the presence of an equally alive yesterday.
—Paul Bowles, *The Worlds of Tangier*, 1958

KISMET IN A BOHO-CHIC SETTING

Imagine the home of well-traveled—and somewhat offbeat—friends, who settled in a desert because it reminded them of another desert they once loved and who built a house like the one they had in that other desert. They filled it with furniture and objects they collected in exotic corners of the world. The result is an eclectic amalgam, but it works. The furnishings mix in a happenstance way, which is odd because the same rule seems to apply to the people who visit: You never know whom you'll meet. Korakia Pensione, in Palm Springs, is that kind of place.

Scottish artist Gordon Coutts had lived for years in Tangier, Morocco, before settling in California. He was fifty-four, and married to a much younger woman who declined the expatriate life, when he built Dar Marroc ("Dar" means "house" in Arabic) in Palm Springs in 1924. Constructed in the Islamic Mughal style, Dar Marroc featured a dramatic cusped-arch entry with hand-carved wooden doors opening into the house, cusped arches on the windows, fountains, an ornate parapet on the roof, and a dome. It had and still has the quality of introversion typical of traditional Arab houses, which present a blank face to the street and offer no clue about the life inside. Their defining feature is the interior courtyard, which not only traps and holds the cooler night air, but is also the inner sanctum of family life, particularly for women and girls, allowing them to be outdoors while protected from wind, sun, and view. For this reason, the architecture

of the courtyard house has been called "the architecture of the veil." By design, an Arab courtyard house is a quintessential hideaway. And, it befits California's Spanish history: Traditional hacienda architecture, with its graceful arches and courtyard gardens, derives from Islamic building precedents brought to Spain from North Africa by the Moors between the eighth and fifteenth centuries.

With Coutts in residence, Dar Marroc was a gathering place for artists, musicians, and celebrities, including painters Agnes Pelton, Nicolai Fenshin, Grant Wood, and Sir John Lavery, weekend painter Winston Churchill, architect Albert Frey, silent-film heartthrob Rudolph Valentino, and character actor J. Carol Nash, Coutts' nearest neighbor. Coutts hung his paintings in the library, where he regaled prospective buyers with tales of his adventures. After he died in 1937, the house fell on hard times. Its dome was removed in the 1950s, and it was mutilated with "improvements," such as dropped acoustical tile hiding the wooden-beamed ceilings, AstroTurf on its wood and stone floors, and aluminum windows.

In 1989, kismet struck. Douglas Smith, another world traveler and admitted raconteur, was drinking retsina at a party on a Palm Springs golf course when he realized how much Palm Springs reminded him of Greece, where he lived in his twenties. A few days later he was staring at the boarded-up doors of Dar Marroc, feeling as though he had just found Mecca. From Dar Marroc's perspective, Smith, an architect and designer, who had completed some 150 historic renovations in southern California, was the perfect owner at the perfect time.

Smith is a lover of vernacular architecture, which he defines as "simply building something with the rocks at your feet and when you get to a tree, go around it." He is of the philosophy that some imperfection is what makes things interesting. He also believes that anything added to an older building with aesthetic character should look like it's always been there. He removed the wrong, and left the right alone. He kept the colorful, chipped Moroccan tiles on the staircase, the heavy wooden beams, the paint-splattered floor in Coutts'

Korakia Pensione
207 South Patencio Road
Palm Springs, CA 92262
760-864-6411
www.korakia.com

Opposite: Near San Jacinto Mountain in Palm Springs, Korakia Pensione, a 1924 interpretation of an Arab house, features a parapet and cusped doors and windows. Palm trees and eclectic furnishings from around the globe give it a bohemian ambience.

studio. For the new, Smith dealt with structure and systems, then with appearances. He trucked in granite naturally stained by the desert climate, used acids on cement floors and walls to achieve a rust color, hired unskilled workers to mix and apply tinted whitewash on the walls, and asked slightly intoxicated palm tree trimmers to dry-lay the stone walls (another deliberate strategy). These touches make Korakia feel like a place that's been worn enough over time to be finally and truly comfortable.

In 1992, having hosted more friends and relatives than he could count, Smith turned Dar Marroc— renamed Korakia (Greek for "crow")—into a

European-influenced pensione. But not just any pensione.

Korakia's furnishings, most of which are handcrafted, come from the Middle East, Europe, and Asia, and resemble a collection acquired in the bazaars and flea markets. Its decoration marries heavy, solid, masculine forms with lighter, flowing elements in a constant interplay of weight and texture, color and light. The combination of these complex elements in this seemingly simple, offhand way requires a keen aesthetic sensibility.

In ambience, too, Smith sought a certain Bohemian sophistication. His café on the Greek island of Spetses was a place where backpackers rubbed elbows with jet-setters and rock stars. He wanted Korakia to be visually stimulating and casual and to function like a house party, where intriguing people would mingle and serendipity would play a part. He started by

This page: Tile roofing and earthenware oil jars, bleach-white walls and luxuriant bougainvillea create textured Mediterranean-inspired vignettes in Korakia's courtyards. Opposite: At twilight, an intimate candlelight dinner for two is set beside one of Korakia's two swimming pools.

offering rooms to dancers and musicians performing nearby. Borrowing a time-tested idea from France's legendary La Colombe d'Or, he encouraged photographers to trade prints for midweek lodging. As a result, Korakia's interiors now showcase works by prominent art and fashion photographers who have stayed there.

Arab houses are rarely built complete, even in urban settings, but grow organically, reaching into adjacent open spaces to meet the needs of subsequent generations. Korakia has grown in a similar way. Its twenty-nine rooms now encompass Coutts' Dar Marroc, J. Carol Nash's Mediterranean-style villa, and Orchard House, a 1918 adobe in a grove of orange trees that is Smith's most recent innovation.

What's happening at Korakia depends upon who's there. You might encounter an alfresco dinner for twenty in the courtyard or an impromptu Cuban dance party. There might be actors and musicians, fashioni- stas and photographers, dancers and painters, writers and publishers, or a group of visiting Tibetan monks cooking in the kitchen. There's a fax machine, because a guest once urgently needed one, but no TV. You can, however, read first editions in the library, watch nighttime screenings of old movies, hike in the San Jacinto Mountains or to the world's largest palm oasis in the Indian Canyons, swim in one of Korakia's two heated pools with mosaic decorations at the bottom, loll on feather beds between soft linen sheets, and relish the deeply satisfying feeling of being, as Smith puts it, "really away."

Opposite: Window hangings are tied casually, opening a path to the pool. This page: An antique buffet holds morning coffee. In a guest room, earthy finishes, subtle lighting, and an intricately carved bed bedecked in white create a sensuous atmosphere.

Lajitas, the Ultimate Hideout

Adventure is just a romantic word for trouble.
—Louis L'Amour

A LUXURY HIDEOUT IN A TEXAS FRONTIER TOWN

Lajitas is the sort of place Louis L'Amour might have chosen as the setting for one of his Western novels. Surrounded by steep canyons, rugged mountains, and desert, it's a resort encompassing an entire Texas frontier town, complete with a historic saloon and trading post, several types of accommodation, restaurants, and shops, along with tennis courts, a golf course, and an airstrip. Sited on a 25,000-acre estate 300 miles from El Paso, Lajitas adjoins Big Bend Ranch State Park to the west and Big Bend National Park to the east. Its colorful history includes Indian raids, Mexican revolutionaries, and cavalry chases.

Lajitas was named by the Spanish in the 1500s for the flat, limestone rocks that form an easy, natural ford on the Rio Grande. In the eighteenth and nineteenth centuries, Comanches and Mescalero Apaches from the north crossed the river and used the San Carlos Trail to raid haciendas and towns in Mexico. In the 1800s, Mexico offered frontier land to Mexican settlers, and by 1880, ranchers from San Carlos formed the core of early settlement in Big Bend. In the 1890s, cinnabar ore, the source of mercury, or quicksilver, was discovered near Terlingua, Texas, and in 1903, the Chisos Mine opened. One of the richest deposits of cinnabar on earth, Chisos made its owner, Howard Perry, from Portland, Maine, a millionaire overnight, and the mine drew almost 2,000 settlers to the area. One was H.W. McGuirk, who bought land for farming. In 1899, he opened Lajitas's saloon, trading post, school, and church, becoming known as "father confessor" along the Rio Grande. He and his wife, Josefa, were the town's first postmasters.

The mine also attracted many Mexican laborers, who came to Big Bend to escape the revolt that had

been going on in their country since 1899. In 1915, U.S. President Woodrow Wilson, who had supported revolutionary forces led by Venustiano Carranza, recognized him as the head of the Mexican government. One of Carranza's rivals, Francisco "Pancho" Villa—cattle rustler, bank robber, revolutionary, ruthless killer, and hero to Mexico's underclasses—trying to provoke war, struck American border towns. Wilson ordered troops commanded by Brigadier General John J. Pershing to patrol the border from the mouth of the Rio Grande in Texas to San Diego, a distance of 1,700 miles. Pershing established the 13th Cavalry outpost at Lajitas. Lajitas's cavalry post accommodations are built on the site of the 1915 army barracks and overlook the original military parade grounds.

"Black Jack" Pershing entered West Point in 1882 at the age of twenty-two. Not among the best and brightest at West Point, he finished thirtieth in his class, but he earned his reputation later in the field. As a young lieutenant, Pershing served in Indian country with the 10th Cavalry, one of two cavalry units (the other being the 9th) and two infantry units (the 24th and 25th) in the segregated U.S. Army, dubbed the "Buffalo Soldiers" by Native Americans. Candidates for the African American units were carefully screened: They were among the best. Pershing wasn't African American, but his admiration for these troops earned him the nickname "Black Jack."

In January 1916, Villa executed seventeen American mining engineers at Santa Ysabel, Mexico. Wilson refused to retaliate, so in March, Villa invaded New Mexico, attacking the 13th U.S. Cavalry and stopping in Columbus for a three-hour spree that left the town in ashes and ten American civilians dead. The 13th chased the marauders, who escaped into the Sierra Madre. Wilson ordered Pershing, who had fought in Cuba and the Philippines, to pursue Villa into Mexico. Black Jack's troops, a combined force of 10,000 men, including the 10th and 13th Cavalries and the 8th Infantry, were supported by aircraft and motorized military vehicles, marking the first time these were used in U.S. warfare.

It was the last cavalry expedition in U.S. military history. Misled through unmapped territory and into

Lajitas, the Ultimate Hideout
HC 70, Box 400
Lajitas, TX 79852
432-424-5000
www.lajitas.com

Opposite: A few miles from the Rio Grande, and near Fort Davis, where the African American units of the U.S. cavalry and infantry were dubbed "Buffalo Soldiers" by Native Americans, a historic fort and Western town have become a deluxe resort.

skirmishes with Carranza's army, Pershing pursued Villa for nearly a year, but with World War I imminent, Wilson ordered the National Guard to secure the border, and sent Pershing to Europe. After the war, Pershing became Army Chief of Staff. His young lieutenant, George S. Patton, became one of the great commanders of World War II, and Captain Charles Young, son of slaves, graduate of West Point, and officer in the 10th Cavalry who had rescued the 13th in Mexico, was promoted to lieutenant colonel, second in command of his regiment. He was the first African American to reach that grade in the regular army. Villa's luck finally ran out in 1923 when he was ambushed. When the

revolution ended, Lajitas again became a quiet farming and trading town.

In the late 1970s, Houstonian Walter Mischer bought Lajitas Resort, envisioning a Palm Springs–style resort. He took over the trading post, created the main street's boardwalk and a golf course, and accurately restored the Santa Maria y San Jose Mission, now the Lajitas Chapel. Still used by several denominations, it boasts adobe construction, beamed ceilings, Saltillo tile flooring, and double wooden doors, along with modern amenities like ceiling fans. Its hand-painted *retablos,* folk art images of saints on punched-tin, were created by a local artist. In 2000, Austin entrepreneur Steve Smith, intrigued by its history and remote location, bought Lajitas at auction, sight unseen.

Lajitas comprises eighty guest rooms in four separate hotels: There are twenty-six units in the cowboy-chic Cavalry Post, decorated with cowhide rugs and rough-worn saddles, and two intimate cabins behind it; "bordello interiors" with iron beds and red-velvet comforters in the Badlands Hotel; twelve rooms and suites surrounding a peaceful courtyard in La Cuesta; and sixteen elegantly rustic junior suites in the Officer's Quarters, which overlook Ambush Golf Course and are steps away from the resort's Agavita Spa, where

This page and opposite: Lajitas's Ambush Golf Course features four holes on an island in the Rio Grande; hole 11A is a par one in Mexico. Accommodations in its historic buildings include bordello rooms in the Badlands Hotel on Main Street.

products and treatments are derived from plants in the Chihuahuan Desert. Lajitas also has a few casita homes with hotel amenities, perfect for groups, couples, and families.

The resort's eighteen-hole Ambush Golf Course, designed by Bechtol Russell, is as unique as Lajitas itself, increasing in difficulty from hole to hole and featuring four holes on an island in the Rio Grande. Hole 11A is a par 1 in Mexico. There's swimming, horseback riding, tennis, hiking, and golf. Guests can go on fossil explorations, identify birds unique to the Big Bend region at Lajitas's La Playa Preserve, or visit historic Fort Davis, established in 1854 to protect gold seekers headed for California from the Kiowas, Comanches, and Mescalero Apaches, and home to the Buffalo Soldiers from 1867 to 1885.

Lajitas's eateries include casual choices at the trading post's deli and the Thirsty Goat Saloon, and elegant

This page: Lajitas's dining rooms and outdoor areas offer comfortable spots to gather and enjoy Texas cuisine. Opposite: Public and guest rooms in the Cavalry Post and Officer's Quarters are studies in Southwest sophistication and cowboy chic.

gourmet dining on west Texas wild game—rattlesnake, jackrabbit, and venison—at the Ocotillo. For some who like it hot, the Candelilla Café serves bold southwestern flavors like Oaxaca molé sauce and poblano peppers, along with the milder five-napkin cheeseburgers. In the evenings, guests enjoy spectacular sunsets over the mountains, live music at the Thirsty Goat Saloon, and movies under the stars at the Lajitas Amphitheater. In these parts, full moons in September and October are still called "Comanche moons."

La Posada Hotel

Standing on a corner in Winslow, Arizona, such a fine sight to see . . . .
—The Eagles

A RESTORED SPANISH COLONIAL REVIVAL MASTERPIECE

La Posada, the hotel Mary Colter, one of the country's first female architects, considered her masterpiece, almost didn't make it to the twenty-first century. And yet there it is, her re-creation of a mid-nineteenth-century Spanish hacienda, near the railroad depot, on a corner of Route 66, in downtown Winslow, Arizona. It didn't always feel as secluded as it does now. In the middle of the action in an increasingly style-conscious town but removed from it, La Posada is like a gorgeous introvert at a party that's just getting started. How the hotel came to be here and how it was saved from demolition and restored is a remarkable tale.

Colter graduated high school in St. Paul, Minnesota, in 1883 at the age of fourteen; at the age of twenty she enrolled in the California School of Design. It was a heady time: California was a wellspring of architectural activity. American architects, including the school's faculty, were drawing on a range of influences and Arts and Crafts ideals to forge home-grown styles. Completing her training in 1890, Colter returned to St. Paul to help support her widowed mother, taught architecture and drawing, became involved in artistic pursuits, and won praise in the newspapers for her decorations at the local armory. Women then were expected to have pastimes, not professions, and architecture was a male-dominated field: In 1900, the U.S. Census counted only one hundred registered female architects.

But, in 1902, having been interested in Native American cultures since childhood, Colter was hired to do a project for the Fred Harvey Company, the concessionaire to the Santa Fe Railroad, which was developing restaurants and hotels in key cities along the railroad from Kansas City westward. She designed a retail center for crafts and home furnishings, called the Indian Building, adjacent to the mission-style Alvarado Hotel in Albuquerque, New Mexico. She then designed Hopi House, the sales center for El Tovar at the Grand Canyon. In 1910, the Santa Fe Railroad and the Harvey Company hired Colter full-time as chief designer, a job she held until she was seventy-nine. She never became a licensed architect. Throughout her forty-six-year career, the Santa Fe Railroad's architects produced and stamped working drawings based on her designs.

Colter designed her first hotel in 1916, just before the United States entered World War I, and building ground to a halt. The postwar years produced a boom in tourism, and hotel plans came off the drawing board and went into construction. The Harvey Company had already developed the marketing theme of showing America to Americans, established an Indian department to source and sell Native American crafts, and localized its hotel designs with Southwestern regional motifs. With her design for El Navajo Hotel in Gallup, New Mexico, which opened in 1918, Colter took this one step further, hiring Navajo craftsmen to create sand paintings, the first permanent installation of these images ever done. The hotel, along with the paintings, was razed in 1957; the Alvarado, along with the Indian Building, in 1970. Colter's Grand Canyon lodgings, Bright Angel Lodge and Phantom Ranch, and elements of her hotel design at La Fonda Hotel in Santa Fe, survived. So has La Posada.

For La Posada, Colter took her historical reference point as 1869, the year of her birth, and imagined the home of a wealthy Spanish don, built when the Southwest was part of Mexico. She created a hacienda compound in the Spanish Colonial Revival style popular in the 1920s. Built of reinforced concrete clad in stucco and featuring red-tile roofs with graceful overhangs, the 78,000-square-foot complex encompasses the hotel, train depot, and retail space. Yet La Posada appears to be a rambling rancho that has grown over time. Colter achieved this by massing a series of two-

La Posada Hotel
303 E. Second Street (Route 66)
Winslow, AZ 86047
928-289-4366
www.laposada.org

Opposite: On Route 66, La Posada, the hotel that architect Mary Colter considered her masterpiece, has been fully restored. Historic black-and-white photos: Colter (right) chatting with guests, in front of the fireplace, and in a posed portrait.

story rectangles with one fortress-style tower and incorporating multiple arches, balconies, and gables. Her detailing is a marvel of heavy-timbered balconies and plank ceilings, Saltillo tile floors, and windows of varied design. Parabolic arches transition between spaces both interior and exterior, including the entry points to the hotel's long central hallway, its lounge, and the Cinder Block Court gallery leading to the bedroom wing. In all, there were seventy rooms, five suites, and grand public spaces, including a large guest lounge and three restaurants.

Colter used local workmen and brought in specialists as needed. To cut and lay stones for the floors, she enlisted Italian stonemasons who had worked on the Roosevelt Dam.

For the hotel's interiors, Colter had walls and ceilings painted in hues of turquoise, burgundy, emerald, and mango with gold and silver accents, hung hand-painted window shades, installed wrought-iron railings and lighting, and commissioned a floral fresco above a staircase. To give visitors the feeling that the hacienda's owners would shortly return, she chose eclectic furnishings a Spanish colonial family might have collected over time. She brought in large comfortable seating and combined it with antiques from Spain and Mexico. From these, and examples of Spanish tile, local artisans in a temporary workshop in the depot made exacting reproductions, down to the worn patina. Colter added decorations—altar pieces adorned with tinsel flowers, confessional stools, Mexican vases wired as table lamps, Navajo rugs, paintings, and whimsical ashtrays on stands, her trademark. She softened the black and white uniforms of the hotel's staff—the famous Harvey Girls, renowned for the professionalism and charm that characterized all of the company's food and hospitality operations—with colorful aprons appliquéd with burros, cacti, and peasants napping beneath sombreros. The Harvey Company published a twelve-page guide to decorative objects in the hotel.

Construction of La Posada began six months before the stock market crash of 1929 that triggered the Great Depression, which was followed by World War II.

This page and opposite: Saltillo tile flooring, graceful parabolic arches, and timbered plank ceilings give La Posada, built in 1929, the look of a circa 1869 Mexican hacienda. Patios and numerous sitting areas are decorated in Southwestern style.

Nonetheless, the hotel had shining moments. Movie stars Clark Gable and Carole Lombard, who took their honeymoon on Route 66, and Jimmy Stewart were guests here. Some of the Harvey Girls who worked at La Posada, in their seventies and eighties now, live in Winslow and recall those days. But, in the years after the war, the car culture took over, and La Posada couldn't compete with new, inexpensive motels.

In 1959, the Santa Fe Railroad closed the building, then turned it into office space, complete with a medical clinic for its employees. La Posada's main building and the depot were left intact, but rooms were gutted, arches filled in, vinyl floors laid, acoustic panel ceilings installed, and white-collar cubicles erected. At least it was still standing. In the late 1980s, however, rumors arose that the railroad was about to vacate the building. Local preservationists, fearing it was a goner, mounted a heroic awareness campaign, convinced the city to maintain the grounds, and secured a federal transportation enhancements grant to help with restoration. In 1994, the National Trust for Historic Preservation placed La Posada on its list of most endangered properties.

Among those who saw that list was Allan Affeldt, a Los Angeles conflict-resolution specialist with a background in architecture, and his wife, well-known artist Tina Mion. Everyone wanted the building to be saved, but federal grant funds could not be released until environmental issues were resolved. Affeldt negotiated with the railroad for three years; its president intervened to develop an agreement. The Federal Highway Administration released the grant funds on the Santa Fe's promise to do the environmental mitigation." Typically you'd have to remove the building to remove the soil to complete the mitigation, and this is not a good preservation technique," Affeldt said. "Everyone was very creative and cooperative to solve this problem." The railroad used high-pressure steam to push oil out of the ground underneath La Posada, a process that took seven years. In 1997, Affeldt was able to purchase La Posada, open for business on a limited basis, and begin restoration.

With the goal of retaining historic fabric and structure, he stripped out changes made in the 1960s to reveal original features, rebuilt vaulted ceilings and arches, repaired plaster, painted, installed new systems, used old photographs and picture postcards to reproduce original details—the list goes on. Estimates placed the cost of restoring La Posada at some twelve million dollars. Federal grant monies amounted to less than 5 percent of that; the rest was privately funded, and everything the hotel earned went into its restoration. Affeldt kept costs down by doing what Colter did. Acting as his own architect—with others to check his work and stamp the drawings—and his own general contractor, he hired a local crew and set up a workshop in the depot.

La Posada's lobby, lounge, ballroom, library, and other public spaces look as they did in Colter's day, and the hotel now has a stylish restaurant, serving gourmet fare like elk medallions, along with updated classics from Fred Harvey restaurant menus. The restored hotel offers fewer guest rooms than La Posada initially did; some small rooms were enlarged. The furnishings are different but assembled in the same way—a blend of reproductions and antiques sourced internationally. Tina Mion's paintings and portraits are decorative focal points in the new interiors. Colter's landscaping plan, her first, was never completed because of the Depression and the war, and the extensive gardens and grounds are a continuing part of the restoration.

Winslow, which suffered mall drain like so many downtowns across America, is enjoying its own revival. The American Orient Express and Amtrak stop there now, bringing tourists once again. And motorists bound for Santa Fe and Scottsdale art galleries, or the Grand Canyon, are happy to exit the interstate and enjoy what this small city has to offer. There are plenty of outdoor activities in the Four Corners area of Arizona too, including hiking, visiting Meteor Crater or a Hopi settlement that is the oldest inhabited community in the United States, rafting, and canoeing past ancient Indian petroglyphs.

Hospitality-industry experts told Affeldt no one would want to stay in a place during restoration. But people appreciated the rare opportunity to watch master craftsmen and witness the re-emergence of Colter's stunning achievement. La Posada's guests are mostly there because they've heard about it from someone they know. It's such a fine sight to see, such a good story to tell.

This page and opposite: Art adds verve to La Posada's colorful interiors. Guest corridors boast original tile flooring and are brightened with paint and punched-tin light fixtures.

La Quinta Resort & Club

It was the kind of place everyone was looking for. It was a wonderful green oasis in the middle of the desert and it was absolutely private.
—Frank Capra

A SHANGRI-LA IN PALM SPRINGS

The first resort in the Palm Springs area was La Quinta. In December 1926, wealthy San Franciscan Walter H. Morgan first welcomed guests to the twenty posh casitas at his elegant and exclusive hotel, located in the Coachella Valley of the Santa Rosa Mountains. Morgan, who suffered from tuberculosis, had moved to the desert for health reasons in 1921 at the age of forty-seven. He purchased 1,400 acres of land that the Cahuilla Indians had called "happy hollow," with the vision of starting a small, exclusive retreat with private casitas offering seclusion and pampering. At a party Morgan hosted, one of his guests described a country house in Mexico surrounded by small cottages and called La Quinta. The name stuck.

In 1925, Morgan hired Gordon Kaufman, a young Pasadena architect, to develop the plans. Kaufman later achieved prominence as the designer of the Los Angeles Times building, the Santa Anita Raceway, and the California Institute of Technology Athenaeum, but La Quinta, for which he received an award from the American Institute of Architects, was one of his first major projects. Kaufman designed the main buildings, lobby areas, open and glassed dining rooms, and guest casitas, along with the furniture and light fixtures that went into them. He grouped the buildings around three courtyards—the hotel entrance, a service area northwest of the lobby, and one interior courtyard, around which were arranged the resort's original guest casitas. He also supervised the landscaping of the hotel's forty-five acres, planting groves of orange, lemon, and grape-

Opposite: Built in the Spanish Colonial Revival style in 1926, La Quinta, the first resort in Palm Springs, quickly became a magnet for generations of movie stars and moguls and helped to define what a resort should be.

fruit trees, towering palms, and stunning flower gardens.

Kaufman brought in Mexican laborers who crafted the more than 100,000 adobe bricks, 60,000 roof tiles, and 5,000 floor tiles that were fired in a kiln on the property and went into the original buildings. The hotel's total construction cost was about $150,000.

From the time it first welcomed a select number of guests with a small but swank dinner dance, La Quinta was a success. Morgan added more casitas and built a golf course—Palm Springs' first—in 1927. His social connections—and well-placed invitations—helped attract an exclusive clientele of moguls such as the Vanderbilts and Duponts, as well as movie stars. The hotel's discreet chauffeurs ferried them over the mountains and through the desert in touring cars equipped with picnic baskets for those inevitable, impromptu interludes while the driver changed a tire that had fallen victim to the rough roads. Greta Garbo, Bette Davis, Dolores del Rio, Ginger Rogers, William Powell, Joan Crawford, Joel McCrea, Marlene Dietrich, Clark Gable, Katharine Hepburn, Richard Widmark, and Ronald Coleman regularly endured the trip to enjoy the seclusion and comfort of La Quinta. During Prohibition, guests gathered around the two fireplaces in the hotel's Santa Rosa Lounge, adding an illicit nip of gin from their hip flasks to the hotel's fresh-squeezed orange juice to create the Orange Blossom cocktail.

Even the stock market crash of 1929 didn't affect the resort's fortunes—in fact, it improved them, as Americans found escape from personal and economic woes at the cinema. La Quinta also weathered Morgan's death in 1931.

In 1934, film director Frank Capra went to the resort for a working vacation, to turn Samuel Hopkins Adams' short story "Night Bus" into a script. The result—*It Happened One Night,* starring Clark Gable and Claudette Colbert—won five Academy Awards, established the romantic-comedy genre, and was the commercial blockbuster that

La Quinta Resort & Club
49-499 Eisenhower Drive
La Quinta, CA 92253
800-598-3828
www.laquintaresort.com

put Columbia Pictures on the map. It was a pivotal event for the American film industry and for Capra, who, from that point on, returned to La Quinta to write movies. *Mr. Deeds Goes to Town, Lost Horizon, You Can't Take It With You, Mr. Smith Goes to Washington,* and *Meet John Doe* were all created at La Quinta.

With the bombing of Pearl Harbor on December 7, 1941, General George Patton and his troops descended upon the desert around Palm Springs to train for combat in North Africa. The Army appropriated area hotels as quarters, offices, and infirmaries. Rationing of gasoline and rubber for tires curtailed travel, and in the spring of 1942, La Quinta closed for the duration of the war. In 1945, it reopened with new owners from Chicago, who included John Balaban, whose brother Barney ran Paramount Studios.

A private airstrip was installed, and once again, celebrated guests began to arrive. The resort grew to encompass 800 guest rooms and suites in Spanish-style casitas with views of the mountains and gardens, forty-one swimming pools and fifty-three whirlpool spas, a 23,000-square-foot spa facility, shops, seven distinctive restaurants including Azure by New York's Le Bernardin, which offers fresh seafood flown in daily, twenty-three tennis courts, and

This page and opposite: La Quinta offers opportunities for socializing and seclusion. Guests can mingle at the main pool, enjoy a private dip outside their casitas, or settle into a lounge chair on an outdoor patio.

ninety holes of golf. These are laid out in five of the country's most fabled golf courses, designed by Pete Dye, Greg Norman, and Jack Nicklaus, and include the PGA WEST® TPC® Stadium Golf® course. A three-year, $60 million renovation completed in 1993 created seventy new spa villas, refurbished all the hotel's interiors, replaced furnishings, created a 1,400-square-foot, two-level playground for children, brought technological capabilities into the twenty-first century—all while maintaining the charm and character that led Capra to call La Quinta his own private Shangri-la.

This page: A traditionally decorated casita interior. Opposite, top: Filmmaker Frank Capra, who called La Quinta his own private Shangri-La, wrote the screenplay for the Academy Award-winning romantic comedy *It Happened One Night* in this casita. Bottom: Architectural details, including Spanish-style roof tiles and beamed ceilings, give character to exteriors and interiors.

The Lodge & Spa at Cordillera

In all probability I am the first woman who has ever stood upon the summit of this mountain and gazed upon this wondrous scene, which my eyes now behold.
—Julia Archibald Holmes, 1858

HIGH ALTITUDE AMENITIES IN THE COLORADO ROCKIES

Julia Archibald Holmes, who at the age of twenty-one became the first woman to scale Pikes Peak, said this in the mid-nineteenth century long before the Colorado Rockies became one of the world's most popular ski destinations, but her sentiment might readily be experienced even today by those lucky enough to enjoy a moment of solitude on an untrammeled mountaintop. The Lodge & Spa at Cordillera, in Edwards, Colorado, located in Vail, the largest ski area in the United States, affords plenty of opportunities for that. It also offers plenty of opportunities to test your mettle on the slopes and four incredible golf courses.

Set atop a private mountain with unsurpassed views of the Vail Valley and the Sawatch Range, the resort is located on a 7,500-acre ranch. The intimate fifty-six-room château-style lodge combines rustic style with pampering comfort and all the outdoor activities Vail has to offer. Its staff focuses on helping guests make every day a memorable experience. In winter, there's downhill skiing just minutes away by resort shuttle to Beaver Creek; the lodge's slope-side ski-in, ski-out Cordillera Club prides itself on being a slope-side concierge, with rental equipment, snacks and hot drinks. Guests can go snowshoeing, snowmobiling, dogsledding, or cross-country schussing at the resort's private Nordic center. In summer, they can swim, play tennis, horseback ride on trails from the equestrian center, go on a cattle drive, ride in a hot-air balloon, go white-water rafting or rappelling in Gore Canyon, hike, mountain bike, or find a spot for

fly-fishing at one of the lodge's private coves on the Eagle River. With music and theater performances in the summer, the Colorado Ski Museum and Ski Hall of Fame, and shopping in Edwards and other Vail towns, the lodge is a year-round destination.

For golf, the lodge boasts a foursome of world-class courses by top designers, reserved for resort guests. For its Mountain Course, Colorado native Hale Irwin transformed the ridges, meadows, and forests of what was once a working ranch into a variety of challenges. Jack Nicklaus' Summit Course, 190 acres on a 9,000-foot mountaintop, is a par 72 course on rolling hills of aspen, sage, and spruce; additional open space provides access for hiking and other activities in the adjacent three-million-acre White River National Forest. Tom Fazio's Valley Course, at a lower elevation, offers wide-open fairways with southern exposure for an extended playing season. And Dave Pelz's short course, at ten holes and all under 130 yards, features tight bunkering, challenging shots, and a terrific valley view.

The Lodge & Spa at Cordillera's main building, characterized by stone construction and comfortable decor, is in the style of a Belgian château, a fitting design—"spa" derives its name from the Belgian town of Spa—as first impressions of the Rockies compared them with the European Alps. Accommodations include comfortable, inviting rooms, suites with fireplaces and balconies, and a variety of mountain-home rentals for longer stays. Interior appointments include Internet access, overstuffed leather chairs, hardwood and tumbled-stone flooring, large wood-cased windows and French doors to private patios offering spectacular views, and hues of gold, sage, and red rock borrowed from the landscape.

The lodge's restaurants present varied menus, decor, and mountain and valley views. The Grouse on the Green boasts authentic pub food, along with microbrewed beers, in authentic interiors designed and built in Ireland; the Timber Hearth Grille, a cozy room with a three-story river-rock fireplace, is the starting point for horse-drawn winter sleigh rides.

The Lodge & Spa at Cordillera
2206 Cordillera Way
Edwards, CO 81632
800-877-3529
www.cordillera-vail.com

The Cordillera Spa, with twelve treatment rooms, greets guests with a twelve-foot carved-glass mural centered between two seven-foot waterfalls. It serves up an extensive selection of body and facial treatments, some incorporating caviar, Kukui coconut, coarse sugars, and ocean salts. Treatments include Swedish and deep-tissue massage for golfers' overworked muscles. Guests can perfect their muscle tone with the spa's eighty-two-foot indoor lap pool, heated outdoor pool, free weights and power-lifting and exercise equipment, and Pilates. Customized wellness programs include nutritional analysis and personal training.

Julia Archibald Holmes arrived in the Rockies just a year ahead of painter Albert Bierstadt, who accompanied an 1859 government expedition led by Colonel Frederick Lander and earned his reputation as a "Western artist" with his paintings on monumental canvases that matched the scale of the landscape. Mount Lander and Mount Bierstadt are east of Vail. Both Bierstadt and Holmes, who scaled Pikes Peak wearing moccasins, bloomers, and a dress considered short by nineteenth-century standards, might have appreciated the spa's skin-reviving High Altitude Rescue. Their mode of travel certainly didn't include any of the amenities the lodge offers.

Holmes, with her husband and two other companions, climbed for four days to reach the 14,110-foot peak. They came, as many did in 1858 and 1859, spurred by the economic crisis of 1857 and the California Gold Rush of 1849, to profit from the large amount of gold discovered in the Rockies. Some of those early prospectors began establishing towns including El Paso, El Dorado, and Colorado City, to provide supplies to gold rushers. In the late 1800s, Frenchman Joseph Brett, attracted by the area's mining potential, established a resort in Edwards for train travelers. Brett, as it happens, had found another source of gold.

About fifty years earlier, Scandinavian immigrants had introduced skiing in the upper Midwest. The sport, which originated in Norway 4,500 years ago, came to the American West during the 1849 Gold

Opposite: The pool's surface is as serene as its setting. This page: The lodge follows the contours of its site. Dining opportunities include a tête-à-tête in the wine cellar and restaurants with year-round views.

Rush. California miners had adopted early skis called "Norwegian Snowshoes," made from pine or spruce and ranging from eight to fourteen feet in length, to traverse the snows of the High Sierra. Before long, miners were competing in impromptu downhill races; soon a racing circuit was established. Betting was heavy, and après-ski parties lasted till dawn. In La Porte, California, in 1874, a skier named Tommy Todd sped eighty-five miles an hour down an icy, 1,800-foot course with a 1,000-foot vertical, an unofficial speed record unmatched until the mid-twentieth century.

Vail was "discovered" in the mid-1950s by rancher Earl Eaton and 10th Mountain Division trooper Peter Seibert, who decided it would be perfect for skiing. In 1962, the U.S. Forest Service granted them a permit for the area's first downhill slopes. Vail is now the largest ski area in North America. At the Lodge & Spa at Cordillera, après-ski parties—complete with fine French wines, microbrewed beers, and massage-relaxed muscles—still sometimes last till dawn.

Best of all, though, is the experience of mastering a new challenge on the slopes or the golf course, on a cattle drive, or in white water. Holmes would have appreciated that. "I have accomplished the task which I marked out for myself," she said. "Nearly everyone tried to discourage me from attempting it, but I believed that I should succeed."

This page: Wooden beams, stone fireplaces, and coffered ceilings (bottom right) are among the lodge's interior details. Opposite: There is a foursome of golf courses, each by a different designer, and an indoor pool with spectacular views.

Mabel Dodge Luhan House

In the desert behind the house, every sagebrush is washed clean and a heavenly smell comes out of the damp, assuaged earth. The rainbow embraces us. We are between its horns. . . . in the lovely lightened air, breathing deep, with a high heart.
—Mabel Dodge Luhan, *Winter in Taos*, 1935

A WORLD REMOVED IN AN ARTISTS' ENCLAVE IN TAOS

Nights at the Mabel Dodge Luhan House are deeply quiet. Though just a ten-minute stroll from Taos Plaza with its art galleries and restaurants, the Luhan House is a world removed, enclosed by adobe walls, bounded on two sides by Pueblo Indian reservation land, a mountain rising behind it, and one boundary marked by a petroglyph-decorated rock placed some 500 years ago by the Tiwa Indians to anchor the sacred energy of the mountain. Ever since it was built in 1918, artists and writers, filmmakers, photographers, musicians, poets, novelists, painters, and social reformers have plied the dead-end road to this retreat. The house's guest list reads like a cultural who's who: Georgia O'Keeffe, D.H. Lawrence, John Marin, Marsden Hartley, Andrew Dasburg, Ansel Adams, Edward Weston, Leopold Stokowski, Dorothy Brett, Paul and Rebecca Strand, Edmund Wilson, Dorothea Lange, Robinson Jeffers, Martha Graham, Laura Gilpin, Bob Dylan, Leonard Cohen, John Wayne, Peter Fonda, Jack Nicholson, Alan Watts.

These artists were drawn by Taos itself, its light, its landscapes, and by the arts community there, which included the house's first owners: socialite Mabel Dodge Luhan, who built it with her fourth husband, Pueblo Indian Tony Luhan, and actor Dennis Hopper, who came to Taos for the making of *Easy Rider* and purchased the house from Mabel's granddaughter in 1970.

The roots of the thriving arts colony at Taos can be

Opposite: New York socialite Mabel Dodge Luhan and her husband, Pueblo Indian Tony Luhan, built their Taos home; it became a stopping point for artists and influentials. Later owned by actor Dennis Hopper, it is now a nonprofit educational center.

traced back to 1898. Young American artists Ernest L. Blumenschein and Bert G. Phillips were on a sketching trip headed from Denver to northern Mexico, when a wheel on their carriage broke on the mountainous road north of Taos. Phillips stayed in Taos; Blumenschein returned every summer until 1919 when he made Taos his permanent home. The two artists founded the Taos Society of Artists. But Taos's art traditions reach back even further: The Pueblo Indians were working with wood, stone, fiber, clay, and leather for nearly 1,000 years by the time Spanish explorers arrived, and Spanish colonists left a rich legacy of decoration and art in their churches and homes. When the two artists arrived, Taos was, as it is now, a land of desert, mountain, and mesa, where high altitude and dry climate produced an intense and clarifying light, where Native American and Spanish peoples maintained their cultural integrity, and where the interaction of cultures produced a singular, creative energy. That is still true. Taos County is home to more than eighty art galleries, and to more than 1,000 artists working in a variety of media.

Mabel Dodge Luhan came to New Mexico in 1917 with her third husband, painter Maurice Sterne, who set up his studio in Santa Fe. Society there was well established; Mabel, whose salon in her Greenwich Village home in New York City had been a magnet for the city's most prominent artists, wanted her own domain. She fell in love with Taos, a frontier town of about 2,000 people, leased a house, saw her first Pueblo Indian ceremonial dance, and experienced an epiphany. As Carl Jung later observed, the Pueblo Indians' fusion of religion and art, work and play, community and individuality, gave them "ample space for the unfolding of personality and permit[ted] them a full life as complete persons." Those qualities, combined with the sensuality expressed in the dance, were just what Mabel had been seeking. On a visit to the reservation, she was invited into the home of an Indian woman, whose husband was seated in the corner playing a flute. It was Antonio Luhan. By 1920 they were together, and in 1923 they married.

In 1918, Tony had persuaded Mabel to build her own

Mabel Dodge Luhan House
240 Morada Lane
Taos, NM 87571
800-846-2235
www.mabeldodgeluhan.com

home. She bought twelve acres bordered by Indian land. For the adobe house, Luhan supervised Mexican and Indian builders, while Mabel designed the interior. "Working with the earth was a noble occupation," she wrote. "To loosen it and make the adobe bricks, mixing the wheat straw...laying them in rows to dry while the rock foundation is being built, and then fitting them carefully upon each other with the rich dark mud between that will turn hard as stone, all of that is a sacred matter, for the wonder of creation is in it, which always seems of greatest significance to the Indians. To take the living earth from under their feet, undifferentiated and unformed, and to shape it into a house...."

Built over a fifteen-year period, the house she called Los Gallos grew to seventeen rooms and 8,400 square feet, and featured a continuous flow of space, openness to air and light, and natural materials. A main room, composed of two rectangles with fireplaces and Mabel's bedroom above it, connected to a dining room that seated about thirty guests. Los Gallos combined ideas from Mabel's Italian villa, such as round steps and long French windows, with local features, including tiles crafted by artist William Henderson, a mural by Pueblo artist Awa Tsireh, and *latilla* ceilings painted in the dining room to look like an Indian blanket. In the 1920s, Mabel added a solarium above her bedroom. By the time it was finished, the compound contained five guest houses, barns, stables, and a 1,200-square-foot gatehouse for staff. Enclosing the huge courtyard were massive gates that incorporated a hand-carved balcony salvaged from a Taos church. A private generator and pump supplied electricity and plumbing. Furnishings combined Southwestern motifs with European antiques. Mabel's large bed, constructed in her room, is still there.

Mabel's creative vision for Taos was that of a sacred center attracting artists and influential individuals who would create the new world order she had intuited by watching the Pueblo Indian dances. They came—most famously, D. H. Lawrence, who painted the windows in the bathroom to create some privacy; Georgia O'Keeffe in her first visits to New Mexico; and Ansel Adams, who was inspired by another guest, photographer

Opposite: Interiors feature *viga* ceilings and vintage furnishings. This page, top: Mabel Luhan's bed was constructed in her room. Bottom: Adobe walls and a fireplace create a comfortable spot in which to read one of Mabel's memoirs of Taos.

Paul Strand. Adams first put his signature style of "soft focus, atmospheric effects, and the simulation of painting" to work in his photographs in *Taos Pueblo*. Novelist Thomas Wolfe, on a cross-country tour, was invited for dinner; when he arrived after midnight roaring drunk, with two women he proclaimed to be of dubious reputation, Mabel refused to descend from her room. Another important guest was John Collier, who became head of the Bureau of Indian Affairs. The Luhans were champions of Indian rights, and, in the early 1920s, led a national campaign against legislation that would have stripped the Pueblos of land and eradicated much of their religion and culture. A practitioner of the philosophy that life itself is the greatest art, Mabel began

writing in the 1930s and produced several memoirs and books about Taos. She died in 1962; Tony, seemingly of heartbreak, died the following year.

In 1970, filmmaker Dennis Hopper bought Los Gallos, renaming it Mud House, and it became a center of the counterculture. In 1977, he sold it to George and Kitty Otero, whose visionary idea of the house's role in the world resembled Mabel's own. The Oteros built an adobe-style guest house with classroom space, held classes, and turned the property into a bed-and-breakfast. Today, owned by the nonprofit Attiyeh Foundation, the Mabel Dodge Luhan House continues to be used in that manner.

There are nine guest rooms in the big house and eight in the guest house, most with fireplaces. All have private baths except for two bedrooms in the main house, which share the D. H. Lawrence bathroom. The gatehouse sleeps four and has two baths, a sitting room, and a working fireplace. In keeping with the Luhan

This page and opposite: Bright white and shots of color energize the home's interiors. English writer D. H. Lawrence, who, with his wife, Frieda, was a frequent guest of the Luhans, painted the bathroom windows to have more privacy.

era, the house has few telephones and no TVs. Mabel's kitchen, still in working order, serves breakfast, and during conferences also prepares lunch and dinner. Designed to satisfy both vegetarian and nonvegetarian tastes, breakfasts—scalloped potatoes and scrambled eggs, sweet-potato enchiladas prepared with tomatillos and green chilies—may be the best in town.

Taos is rich in arts and outdoor activities. With elevations ranging from 5,000 feet to nearly 14,000 feet and a network of irrigation ditches, it boasts verdant views and all kinds of warm- and cold-weather sports. In winter there's Alpine and cross-country skiing, snowboarding, snowshoeing, and snowmobiling. In summer, guests can bike, rock climb in New Mexico's highest mountains, hang glide, raft or kayak, fish for trout, and hike in one of several wilderness and recreation areas. Golfers can choose from two nine-hole and two championship eighteen-hole golf courses. Taos has six museums: three art museums showing the work of Taos

artists, and three house museums, including the homes of frontiersman Kit Carson and Ernest Blumenschein. There's an active cultural schedule, and workshops in a variety of media at the Taos Institute of Arts and Taos Art School. There might even be a class, like one of Natalie Goldberg's creativity or writing workshops, at the Mabel Dodge Luhan House.

The artists who started it all are at the Taos Pueblo, the only living Native American community designated both a UNESCO World Heritage Site and a National Historic Landmark. Continuously inhabited for more than 1,000 years, the Pueblo structures look much as they did in 1540 when Spanish explorers thought they had found one of the fabled golden cities of Cibola. They were not the last to believe that. For those who measure their wealth in creative output rather than coinage, Taos may indeed be a city of gold.

Mahakua, Hacienda de San Antonio

I am a man. Little do I last. And the night is enormous.
But I look up. The star is right. Unknowing, I understand.
I too am written, and at this very moment, someone
spells me out.
—Octavio Paz, "Brotherhood"

A GRACIOUS MEXICAN ESTATE UNDER THE VOLCANO

Mahakua, Hacienda de San Antonio, in Comala, Mexico, about 124 miles south of Guadalajara and seventeen miles north of the state capital Colima City, boasts two magnificent fireplace mantels carved of black volcanic stone in the nineteenth century. Where did the stone come from? One of two places. As its neighbors, Mahakua claims two towering volcanoes: the inactive, snowcapped El Nevado de Colima and the smoke-and-lava-spewing Volcán de Colima, sometimes called El Volcán de Fuego, or fire volcano, the most active volcano in Mexico.

The hacienda, located in the high country of western Mexico, was built between 1879 and 1890 by Don Arnoldo Vogel, a German coffee and sugar planter, and his Mexican wife, Clotilde Quevedo de Vogel, who named their *casa grande* Hacienda de Santa Cruz. The Spanish brought the feudal hacienda system to Mexico, appropriating Indian lands to establish vast land holdings. As they grew, haciendas supplied the needs of their communities, including food, clothing, and medical treatment. From 1876 to 1911, dictator Porfirio Díaz encouraged capitalism and foreign investment, offering land for new haciendas and enlarging existing ones. Vogel took advantage of this policy, establishing his estate in the cool highlands ideal for growing Arabica coffee. At the peak of its prosperity, the plantation extended almost to the Pacific coast, and its coffee was exported worldwide.

Though built in the late nineteenth century, the resort's historic main building incorporates a variety of architectural influences. Elements of Spanish architecture—porticoed galleries of one and two stories, courtyards, arches—trace their roots to ancient Rome and to the Moors who invaded the Iberian Peninsula in 711. Christian kingdoms in the north gradually drove the Moors southward, but the last Moorish kingdom, Granada, wasn't conquered until 1492. When the Spanish colonized Mexico and islands in the Caribbean and , they brought this building tradition with them. Mexico first won its independence from Spain in 1821, but in 1864, Napoleon III installed Maximilian I, an Austrian archduke of the Hapsburg family, and his wife, Carlota, as emperor and empress. The Mexicans executed him in 1867, but the French influence in architecture and culture remained. By the nineteenth century, hacienda architecture in Mexico had reached the apex of opulence and incorporated Mudéjar (as Spanish rendition of Moorish design is called), Romanesque, Gothic, and Baroque elements into the Neoclassical style. All that is evident here.

Mahakua's living and dining rooms feature fifteen-foot brick barrel-vaulted ceilings in the Romanesque style. Their floors are a grid work of wood planks enclosing red tiles. Imposing fireplace mantels are carved of black volcanic rock. Floor-to-ceiling, transomed French doors admit light, air, and the rustle of coconut palms in the breeze. The living room features a modern hand-carved table inlaid with silver talismans and proportioned to match the mantel. The hacienda's Mirador Room, named after the Spanish-Arab lookout tower and located on the roof terrace, is a fine place to admire the view or watch satellite TV.

The hacienda's richly appointed twenty-five guest suites are located in a two-story wing with a sweeping staircase of volcanic stone. Each suite is crowned by a high, vaulted ceiling and features French doors and windows, a fireplace, and a terrace or balcony opening to a courtyard garden. Interiors are themed to the region's tapestries, its *charreada* horsemen, pre-Columbian legends, and Spanish motifs. Mahakua's 1,350-square-foot Grand Suites—Volcán, Sol, and Quetzal—boast large living rooms and interiors that reflect the lifestyle of a gracious country mansion. The

Mahakua,
Hacienda de San Antonio
Municipio de Comala
CP 28450, Colima, Mexico
800-624-2582
www.mahakua.com

Opposite: Mahakua's late nineteenth-century Neoclassical hacienda is an elegant composition rooted in Spanish and Moorish traditional architecture. On this resort, working plantation, and ranch near Mexico's most active volcano (bottom left), riders pass an arched Roman-style aqueduct.

twenty-two smaller hacienda suites are also decorated on a grand scale with tapestries, hand-woven carpets and draperies, carved mirrors, original paintings, and ceramic lamps.

In 1904, Vogel built an arched Roman-style aqueduct of volcanic stone to draw water from the El Cordoban River and to generate power for electricity and the ranch's agricultural machinery. It still provides water for the hacienda and gardens.

When El Volcán de Fuego erupted in 1913, causing heavy ash flows and forming a crater more than 900 feet deep, the plantation remained unscathed. The grateful Clotilde built a chapel dedicated to Saint Anthony. Its Neoclassical interior is a triumph, detailed with vaulted ceilings, broken-arch pediments, heavy cornices, dentil decoration, and fluted columns surmounted by gold Ionic and Corinthian caps. Seating sixty, it still welcomes worshipers from surrounding communities during special festivals.

The hacienda's gardens were inspired by Granada's Alhambra Palace, built by a Moorish king as a recreation of paradise on earth. Here grow cypresses, fig trees, vanilla plants, oak trees with hanging moss, mango, guava, papaya, and nut trees, as well as the blue agave used to make tequila.

The restored hacienda is sited on 470 acres within a 5,000-acre working ranch. Its 300-acre organic coffee plantation uses processes from the 1880s; growing, harvesting, and fermentation are virtually machine-free. Its organic farm supplies produce for the kitchen, and its dairy farm produces Gouda, Asiago, cheddar and goat cheeses. The hacienda offers many spots in which to enjoy a meal by day or candlelight, whether it's in the grand dining room or pool pavilion, on its terraces, in its intimate gallery or the guest rooms.

Despite Mahakua's elegant comfort, it has not always been the place it is now. During the 1910–1921 Mexican Revolution, when haciendas were pillaged and seized, Mahakua was spared only because the owners flew a German flag and threatened to kill any

interlopers. Even so, it eventually fell into disrepair. In the 1970s, a group of French and Mexican architects began renovations, and a 1980s expansion replicated the hacienda's original architectural style. Restoration resumed in the mid-1990s when a crew of interior designers, craftsmen, artists, ceramists, botanists, and builders transformed it into a private estate. In October 2000, it was opened to guests as Amanresort.

In addition to the resort amenities one might expect—lighted tennis court, swimming pool, mountain biking, and hiking—the ranch offers horseback riding on its own 5,000 acres through vistas of lakes, volcanoes, mountains, and a grove of overarching one-hundred-foot bamboo plants. There's a corral where Mexican *charreadas*, or demonstrations of horsemanship, are held and an amphitheater for music and drama performances. Nature walks include hikes led by a vulcanologist through a hidden "volcano trail."

This area of Mexico holds a wealth of treasure that the Spanish conqueror Cortez never would have

appreciated. In nearby Comala, called "the white city," the plaza is a jewel box of outdoor cafés, craft shops, and strolling mariachi musicians. Farther up the mountain, the village of Suchitlan is famous for its mask makers and exorcisms; on the road is a spot where objects seem to roll uphill. Colima, the state capital, was a pre-Columbian metropolis long before the Spanish founded a town there in 1523. Called the "city of palm trees," it boasts colonial-style buildings, many rebuilt after a 1941 earthquake; museums with pre-Columbian art, including the potbellied dog common to the burial sites in the area; theater and folkloric ballet performances; annual bullfights and festivals; and archaeological sites. On the coast, Manzanillo offers world-class sail fishing; and at Boca

This page and opposite: The hacienda was impeccably restored by French and Mexican architects in the 1970s. Its pink exteriors, including this rooftop sitting area and porticoed courtyard, are defined by black volcanic stone pillars and trim.

de Pascuales, surfers find ten-foot walls of white water, powerful waves breaking left and right, and some of the fastest, biggest, and hollowest tubes in Mexico—not a place for novices.

Climbing either the active El Volcán de Fuego or the extinct volcano, snowcapped El Nevado de Colima, requires physical stamina, mountaineering experience, and special information. There is a guided hike part-way up the benign 14,300-foot Nevado de Colima, the centerpiece of Nevado National Park, a nature reserve that is home to more than twenty rare and endangered species in varied landscapes at different elevations. El Volcán de Fuego is classified as a high-risk volcano and is closely monitored. It lets off pressure with earthquakes and tremors, explosions, pyroclastic eruptions, sulfuric emissions, ash falls, volcanic mud flows, firestorms that pelt its slopes, and plumes reaching as high as three miles. Climbing to its 13,000-foot summit crater is not advised. To view it, Mahakua recommends going to Yerbabuena not far from the resort.

El Volcán de Fuego has catastrophic eruptions about every hundred years, and scientists say it is now in a climactic phase. Because it is Mexico's most active volcano, people come from around the world to see it. Mahakua, Hacienda de San Antonio is in its shadow. As Mexican poet Octavio Paz wrote, "Little do I last. And the night is enormous." In the meantime, here and now, under the watchful eye of Saint Anthony, life can be good.

This page and opposite: Interiors boast Romanesque barrel-vaulted ceilings; in the dining and living rooms, fifteen-foot ceilings are brick, floors are wooden and tiled, and mantels are made from black volcanic rock.

The Murray Hotel

Now the tourist or businessman makes the journey in palace cars, and there is nothing to remind him of the danger or desolation of Border Days.
—W.F. Cody, "Buffalo Bill"

A MAIN STREET MONTANA CLASSIC NEAR YELLOWSTONE

The small-town hotel was once an American institution, on a main street, a place where locals could gather, and folks passing through could stop for a meal, or overnight, or a longer stay. The Murray Hotel in Livingston, Montana, population 7,500, give or take a few, is such a hotel—the Northern Pacific Railway's original "stopping off" point for visitors to Yellowstone National Park, the world's first national park. The railroad discontinued passenger service in the late 1970s, but Livingston, bisected by Highway 89 and about a forty-five minute drive from the park's north entrance, is a treasure, a place made for strolling, with neighborhoods of antique houses, a downtown of restored classic turn-of-the-century brick buildings, shops and restaurants, art galleries, museums, and an impressive train depot that recalls the days when rail was the most elegant way to travel.

Behind the Murray Hotel's brick façade and neon sign is a lobby opulently appointed with copper, tile, wood, and marble, captivating details that have been erased in so many small-town buildings across America. A stairway leads to a stylish mezzanine, the rich woodwork gleams, simple electric chandeliers of white glass hang overhead, and a venerable hand-cranked Otis elevator awaits behind its metal grate to deliver guests to one of the hotel's twenty-six guest suites. In restoring this circa 1904 gem, its owners, Dan and Kathleen Kaul, had the good sense to remove eyesores—like barn-board partitions, shag carpet, and acoustical tile ceilings—and leave the original alone. They augmented the hotel's period style with antiques like oak four-poster beds, and added comfortable chairs upholstered in chintz fabrics.

While retaining turn-of-the-last-century charm, they added turn-of-this-century amenities. Each of the two-, three-, and four-room guest suites has its own bath featuring a vintage tub, a wet bar equipped with a microwave and refrigerator, a telephone with Internet connection, controls for air conditioning and heat, and at least one cable TV. The 2nd Street Bistro, the hotel's restaurant, is one of south central Montana's best, serving hearty food, including fresh-caught local trout. Add that to the list of the Murray's charms, along with the pleasures of a main street in an out-of-the-way town under the big sky.

Under that big sky, the area around Livingston is rich in opportunities for outdoor activities. Anglers come from around the world to cast for wild trout in area rivers and streams—and to consult with the experts at Dan Bailey's Fly Shop, a local institution. Besides the fishing itself, the International Fly Fishing Center, operated by the Federation of Fly Fishers, features aquariums of live fish; an astonishing collection of thousands of antique and modern flies, fly rods, and fishing accessories; and a research library and art collection. Murray guests can take free fly-casting lessons, and there are fly-fishing day camps for kids. Livingston is also within easy reach of skiing on the Absaroka Range, the lush Paradise Valley, white water rafting, horseback riding, and myriad other sports.

The first to fish the waters around here were Native Americans who moved along the Yellowstone River more than 4,000 years ago. Their descendants are the Bannock, Blackfeet, Flathead, Shoshone, and Absaroka Crow tribes. In 1803, the United States acquired south-central Montana in the Louisiana Purchase. In 1806, Lewis and Clark's reports of the territory's natural resources attracted trappers, traders who began the first trading post on the river in 1827, and prospectors, who established Montana's first mines.

In 1864, as Montana mines were going into production, President Lincoln signed a law granting the Northern Pacific Railroad 47 million acres to build

The Murray Hotel
201 West Park
Livingston, MT 59047
406-222-1350
www.murrayhotel.com

Opposite: On Main Street, in Livingston, Montana, once the Northern Pacific Railroad's gateway to Yellowstone National Park, the restored circa 1904 Murray Hotel retains the flavor of the elegant small-town railroad hotel, and welcomes cowboys, real and imagined.

a northern Pacific route. Philadelphia financier Jay Cooke purchased the railroad in 1869, financing its construction through the sale of bonds. There was in the West, Cooke's publicists said, a "vast wilderness waiting like a rich heiress to be appropriated and enjoyed." Yellowstone was part of that wilderness.

In 1871, *Scribner's Monthly* accepted an article about Yellowstone by Nathaniel P. Langford, a friend of Cooke's who later became the park's first superintendent. Thomas Moran, *Scribner's* chief illustrator who created the artwork for the article, decided to see Yellowstone's wonders himself. He joined an 1871 expedition led by renowned geologist Ferdinand Vandeveer Hayden, one of the four great western surveys sponsored by the U.S. Geological Service and the Department of the Interior. The expedition also included famed landscape photographer William

This page: The Absaroka Mountain Range and many local streams offer myriad outdoor activities, including some of the best fly-fishing in the West. Opposite: The Murray Hotel's lobby and mezzanine have survived the passage of time virtually intact.

Henry Jackson, the first to capture the wonders of Yellowstone on film. Moran's watercolors and paintings and Jackson's photographs helped persuade Congress to set aside some 2.2 million acres as Yellowstone National Park in 1872. A short time later, Congress purchased Moran's monumental painting *The Grand Canyon of the Yellowstone*, to hang in the U.S. Capitol.

In 1880, just as coal was discovered around Livingston and shipping coke and ore became important, a group of German and American investors, led by German immigrant Henry Villard, took control of the Northern Pacific. A journalist and financier, Villard covered the Lincoln-Douglas debates, the Pikes Peak Gold Rush, and the Civil War, married the daughter of abolitionist William Lloyd Garrison, ran the Oregon and California Railroad and the Oregon Steamship Company, oversaw completion of the Northern Pacific's transcontinental line, and went on to found General Electric. Villard's eastern "immigration bureau" attracted 30,000 settlers to Oregon; his New York townhouses survive as a museum.

By 1882, Chinese, Mormon, Irish, and Swedish construction crews were laying about a mile and a half of track a day across Montana. The railroad sent thirty freight wagons drawn by 140 oxen and loaded with 140,000 pounds of merchandise to establish a supply store in Livingston for the construction crews. Residents of a downriver encampment moved to the site, and the new town flourished with six general stores, two butcher shops, two drug stores, two hotels, one hardware store, two restaurants, two watchmakers, three blacksmiths, two wholesale liquor dealers, and thirty saloons. But Northern Pacific officials had planned a town named Livingston a short distance to the northwest, so the entire town of 500 people relocated. In 1883, the railroad built a huge locomotive repair complex, which under different ownership still services locomotive and freight cars. By 1889—when Montana became a state—Livingston was prospering.

To welcome Yellowstone-bound passengers in grand style, the Northern Pacific built Livingston's impressive depot in 1902; it's now a museum and cultural center, a short mosey from the hotel.

The Murray opened in 1904. Called the Elite Hotel, it was elegant lodging for railroad travelers. The family of Montana Senator James E. Murray bankrolled

its first owner, Josephine Kline, who, by 1922, had accomplished the hotel's first and only expansion—to four floors. In 1925, the Murrays foreclosed and took over, renaming it the Murray Hotel. Throughout the 1920s and '30s, the Murray was one of the grandest hotels in the Northwest, a watering hole and rendezvous for the elite.

The development of the interstate highway system in the 1960s and the end of passenger rail service in the late 1970s sent the Murray into obscurity—but not into decline. In 1978, Cliff and Pat Miller, a Livingston rancher and his wife, bought the hotel at auction. Its current owners, Dan and Kathleen Kaul, a Minneapolis building contractor and restaurant manager, discovered the Murray during a ski trip in 1990. Its years out of the limelight helped preserve the hotel's original features and make it so ready for its close-up now.

A century old, the Murray is a classic, attracting a heady mix of cowboys (real and imagined), tourists, backpackers, fishermen, and that very special class of people who are well known but couldn't care less. Its guest register records visits from Buffalo Bill Cody; Martha Canary aka Calamity Jane, who was later accommodated at the Livingston jail; humorist Will Rogers, who tried to bring a saddle horse up in the 1905 Otis elevator; writer Richard Brautigan, whose *Trout Fishing in America* had nothing whatever to do with the sport; and famous—and infamous— film director Sam Peckinpah, who lived here for a while; a sign on the door to his suite said, "The ol' iguana sleeps and the answer is no." Discerning guests quickly recognize that lack of pretension is one of the Murray's fundamental charms.

It may not pose the danger or desolation of Border Days, but "This isn't a façade," Kathleen Kaul says. "This is the real West."

This page and opposite: The Murray Hotel's guest rooms and dining room marry turn-of-the-century appointments with modern conveniences in a location within easy walking distance of the town's railroad depot and other museums, Dan Baily's Fly Shop, and the International Fly Fishing Center.

Orbit In's Palm Springs Oasis & Hideaway

A little study of this plan is almost bound to impress one with the idea that here indeed is a new way of life, at least for those times when one craves a real rest. One gets interested, too, in the owner's way of life in this new concept of a building venture.
—*Architectural Record*, 1948

SPACE AGE MODERNISM AND SAKE MARTINIS IN THE CAPITAL OF COOL

In 1948, when *Architectural Record* reported on the Town and Desert Apartments, Modernism was the next new thing in Palm Springs. Not only was it avant-garde architecture, it represented new ideas of casual sophistication—how space should be divided and used, how everyday objects should look, and how people, in an era of prosperity, technological triumph, and space exploration, could live, entertain, and enjoy their leisure time. Designed by Herbert W. Burns, a builder and innkeeper who built a number of small inns and private homes in Palm Springs during the 1940s and '50s, Town and Desert Apartments lives on as the Hideaway, one of the Orbit In's two boutique hotels. Avant-garde has, inevitably, become retro, and in a town that's a preservationist's paradise of mid-twentieth-century style, no place does it better than the Orbit In.

The Orbit In's nine-room Hideaway and nine-room Oasis inns are located a short walk away from one another and from the heart of the village. Cocktail hour, featuring the sake "Orbitinis" that have become a hotel trademark, takes place at the Oasis's poolside, lava lamp lit–Boomerang Bar. Hideaway guests stroll over for it–or not. The groovy atmosphere, complete with a cocktail mix of rice crackers and nuts in '50s Melmac bowls, inspires people to don vintage RayBan sunglasses, slick back their hair, and dance barefoot to Sinatra crooning "Fly Me to the Moon" on the Orbit's custom soundtrack.

The Orbit In's architecture and ambience sum up the Modernist vision of a better lifestyle. After World War II, a spirit of experimentalism, an infusion of money from people drawn by the climate, along with new manufacturing processes and standardized building components innovated for the war effort, made the West fertile territory for Modernist design that had emerged early in the twentieth century. Frank Lloyd Wright had completed his first California project in 1909. In 1917, internationalist Le Corbusier published his influential *Towards a New Architecture*. And, in 1919, Walter Gropius founded Germany's Bauhaus school, a design workshop unifying art and technology, the fine and applied arts, function and aesthetics. It was a new way of thinking about buildings. "The Bauhaus believes the machine to be the modern medium of design," Gropius said. When the Nazis closed the school in 1933, leading Modernists came to the United States. They and their American counterparts innovated buildings unconventional in design, construction, and use of materials. The emphasis was on technical perfection, fine proportions, and regularity rather than symmetry. For the first time, thin steel columns supported walls of glass and roofs that seemed to float. Planes and surfaces were thin, natural materials were used in new ways, style was achieved by structure rather than ornamentation, and glass walls created a seamless flow between interior and exterior space.

Burns' contemporaries in Palm Springs included industrial designer Raymond Loewy; the great architectural photographer Julius Shulman; Richard Neutra, who created a south California regional style with buildings that extended pinwheel fashion into the landscape; Donald Wexler, who designed the Palm Springs airport and the "steel homes" in north Palm Springs; and Albert Frey, one of the first of Le Corbusier's disciples to build in America. Neutra's 1946 Desert House in Palm Springs was designed for the Kaufmann family, who had commissioned Wright to design their home, Fallingwater, in Pennsylvania. It still stands, as does most of Frey's work, which includes Palm Springs City Hall, the Palm Springs Desert Museum, and the second of the houses he designed for himself, now part of the museum.

Orbit In's Palm Springs
Oasis & Hideaway
562 W. Arenas (Oasis)
370 W. Arenas (Hideaway)
Palm Springs, CA 92262
877-996-7248
www.orbitin.com

Opposite: In the village of Palm Springs, close to the San Jacinto Mountains, the Orbit In is a celebration of Modernist architecture and design, a place where guests dance barefoot to Sinatra crooning "Fly Me to the Moon."

Burns designed Town and Desert Apartments in 1947. The jagged L-shaped plan that stretches horizontally into the landscape included his home and office, and five rental units. A decade later, he designed the Oasis. Like the Hideaway, it was a collection of apartments around a pool, featuring strong horizontal lines and low-pitched roofs with deep overhangs. Burns achieved a flow between the indoor and outdoor spaces with floors that sit flat to the land, glass walls, natural materials, and a palette of desert hues.

The Orbit In's owners, Oregon residents Christy Eugenis and Stan Amy, first saw the Oasis property while on vacation in Palm Springs. Eugenis, out Rollerblading, happened to see the "For Sale" sign in front of the rundown motel, which still had its vintage sign and name, the Village Manor. "All they'd ever done was paint and recarpet," she said. "They hadn't touched any of the original features—and that's almost impossible to find." They bought the Oasis in early 1999 and opened it in 2001, after nearly two years of renovations. In 2001, they bought the Hideaway, which then resembled a seedy set straight out of film noir; it opened in 2003. Under the guidance of architect Lance O'Donnell, of the firm O'Donnell and Escalante, who grew up in a Modernist house near Palm Springs, both properties received restorations that are ring-a-ding-ding on

target, right down to the last Eames chair. "Most of my friends like to stay in small hotels, and I've always loved the '50s because of the colors and the amoeba and geometric shapes," Eugenis said. "I spotted a trend."

Eugenis and O'Donnell updated systems, improved landscaping and amenities, and carefully showcased features that were miraculously still intact. Among the original features are white enamel kitchenettes, baths tiled in pink, baby blue, and mint green, combed plywood accent walls, recessed wall clocks, soffits above all the picture windows, and vertical poles and ledges. Restoration in both hotels adhered to the original details and incorporated imaginative adaptations consistent with Burns' designs. When electric heaters were removed, their niches were converted into magazine racks. While fixing the wall clocks, workers found the label 'American Clock Co.' The company, still in existence, still had the clock templates designed for Burns' properties. Eugenis bought an assortment in aluminum.

The Oasis's pool was moved four feet from its original location to allow construction of a privacy wall topped with Carolina cherry plants. A new terrazzo poolside bar inlaid with pieces of colored glass, crafted by a Seattle artist, and nicknamed the Boomerang Bar, is equipped with Internet plug-ins at the base of its glowing lava lamps. A colorful perforated metal-shade structure is equipped with misters to render the temperature some twenty degrees cooler than it is in the sun. It's a terrific place to relax in a 1966 Richard Schultz lounge chair, sip an Orbitini, and admire the San Jacinto Mountains.

This page: Night at the Oasis pool bar. Afternoon at the Hideaway pool. Opposite, top row: The Rat Pack suite displays '60s furnishings and a photo of Frank, Dean, and Sammy. Bottom row: The Bertoia suite contains furniture Harry Bertoia himself designed.

For furnishings, Eugenis—a first-time hotel owner who's had multiple careers as a real-estate agent, photo stylist, sportswear designer, and purveyor of vintage clothing—scoured secondhand stores, haunted estate sales, and tapped resale dealers in modern furnishings to find authentic furniture by Eero Saarinen, Charles and Ray Eames, Harry Bertoia, Jens Risom, Pierre Paulin, Marcel Breuer, and Isamu Noguchi, among others. A collection of Aimes Aire furniture surrounds the Hideaway's pool. Modern pieces, like Blue Dot storage units, Jamaica bar stools by Spanish designer Pepe Cortez, and mid-century designs by Herman Miller and Knoll are also part of the mix. Ray Eames fabric introduced in 1999 was used for window treatments custom-made by a draper who had been working in Palm Springs for fifty years. New sea grass floor coverings complete the buildings' original indoor-outdoor concept and provide an eye-soothing backdrop for furnishings.

Both hotels offer suite accommodations with kitchenettes and either private or poolside patios. Vintage tunes supply in-room CD players, and TVs equipped with VCRs show classic and current movies from the Orbit In's library. Each suite is themed with wit and individuality, and swings in neutrals with shots of Rose's Lime, Rhum Orange, and Blue Curacao. At the Oasis, the Rat Pack Suite features photos of Frankie, Dean, and Sammy; Bertoia's Den has an original Bertoia bird chair and ottoman; and the Leopard Lounge is just what one would expect from its name. There's also the Atomic Paradise Room, where decor includes a 1958 Orange Slice chair by Pierre Paulin, a 1948 ball clock, and Blue Dot's 1999 Modulicious cabinet; and the Albert Frey lounge, where photos of him hang on the wall, cabinets were inspired by those in his home, and the outdoor shower, privately enclosed behind a bougainvillea-draped wall, affords a view of the mountainside where Frey's house stands.

Julius Shulman's photographs, for the 1948 *Architectural Record* article, guided restoration and furnishing decisions at the Hideaway. Appropriately, they decorate its interiors. The black and white images look uncannily similar to the way the hotel looks today: cool, elegant, and the furthest thing from kitsch.

"In Orbit" spa services leave guests feeling as pampered as Doris Day; *Leave It to Beaver*–style cruiser bikes are available for a spin through town; the San Jacinto Mountains tempt guests to lace up those sneakers and hit the trail; and the two pools are invitations to throw caution to the wind and perfect a tan. The Orbit In is the kind of place that reminds one that while California is a state of the union, it is also a state of mind.

This page: A sleek guest lounge and a 1948 ball clock. Opposite: The Leopard Lounge features an authentic Isamu Noguchi coffee table and a 1950s swivel circle chair upholstered in—what else—leopard. Outside is a private patio.

Rancho de la Osa Guest Ranch

A VENERABLE HACIENDA IN THE LUSH SONORAN DESERT

Rancho de la Osa, one of the last great Spanish haciendas in America, has stood in the rolling grasslands of the high Sonoran Desert on the Mexican border for so long it seems to have grown here. The natural beauty of the Altar Valley, Baboquivari Mountain, and the nearby Buenos Aires National Wildlife Refuge invite hiking, riding, and exploring, just to become a student of nature for a while.

Located in Sasabe, Arizona, near the 7,830-foot granite peak of Baboquivari, which the Papago Indians believe to be "the center of mother earth," Rancho de la Osa traces its roots to the late seventeenth century, when Spanish Jesuits built a mission outpost here. One of their early adobe buildings, constructed about 1725 and used for more than a century as a trading post by local Indians and Mexicans, is still in use. It's now the ranch's cantina, a favorite watering hole, serving tequila from its antique Mexican bar, where it's easy to feel like a throwback to the Old West.

Rancho de la Osa is one of those places that helped shape people's impressions of the Old West—starting with Victor Fleming's 1925 silent film, *Son of His Father*, about saving 'La Rosas Ranch' from foreclosure, which was filmed here. Among the ranch's guests were Western author Zane Grey, cowboy actor Tom Mix, and the late, great John Wayne, quoted in his wife Pilar's autobiography as saying, "The only time I get on a horse is when I make a movie."

Opposite: Rancho de la Osa, one of the last great Spanish haciendas in North America, traces its earliest building to 1725. Here in the high Sonoran Desert, the only place where Saguaro cacti (bottom left) grow, the landscape is lush with vegetation and wildlife.

Rancho's past is populated by a cast of characters as colorful as any film, and it's the real deal.

In 1812, the ranch was part of a three-million-acre land grant to the Ortiz family of Mexico. Legend has it that during the Mexican Revolution, Pancho Villa fired on the Ortiz hacienda. (Truth or tale, a Mexican cannonball from that era was found embedded in Rancho's walls.) At the end of the Mexican-American War, when the 1853 Gadsden Purchase established the border, Rancho fell into U.S. territory. An 1886 land survey described it succinctly: "A ranch house and out buildings. Land rolling, soil third and fourth rate, good grass. No timber."

Taking advantage of that good grass, Colonel William Sturgis made the 1725 mission the center of the ranching empire he called Rancho de la Osa, meaning "the bear." In the years of the great cattle drives, Sturgis' cowboys herded about 50,000 head a year up from Mexico. Made rich by longhorns, the cattle baron spared no expense in renovating the adobe hacienda.

The *Arizona Daily Star* reported in 1889, "The floor is of inlaid wood, carried, as most of the material...from Tucson, a distance of eighty miles...the material for the floor was shipped there from Europe. The windows in the hall are stained glass, also imported. The rest of the hacienda...is in keeping with this magnificence." The article described the ranch's layout: two quadrangles—one a courtyard housing servants at the rear of the main house, the other housing ranch workers and centered on a ten-acre garden.

After Sturgis, Rancho had a number of owners. These included a man who bequeathed a single gold piece instead of the ranch to a son whom he called "a vicious criminal and a disgrace to his family," and another who battled to keep the land when Arizona became a state in 1912, and prevailed. In 1921, John and Louisa Wade Wetherill, considered two of the foremost historians of the Southwest, began Rancho's transformation into one of America's premier guest ranches. The Wetherills were among the first Anglos to trade with the Navajo. By the 1880s, the DinÂ, as

Rancho de la Osa Guest Ranch
P.O. Box 1
Tucson/Sasabe, AZ 85633
800-872-6240
www.ranchodelaosa.com

the Navajo are now known, their subsistence threatened by diminishing numbers of wild game and potential crop failures, began to emphasize the sale of their woven blankets and rugs. The Wetherills established a trading post near Chaco Canyon, then moved to remote Olijato, Utah. Louisa learned the Navajo language, earned the friendship of tribal leaders, and documented their culture in a 1934 book, *Traders to the Navajos: The Wetherills of Kayenta*, written with Frances Gillmor.

In 1927, Kansan Arthur Hardgrave bought the spread as a birthday present for his wife, who continued it as a guest ranch, adding lion and jaguar hunting to its roster of activities. In 1935, a group of absentee investors, including U.S. Treasury Secretary Henry Morgenthau Jr. and William Clayton, U.S. Undersecretary of State, who in 1948 would draft the Marshall Plan in one of the casitas, bought the property. Guests, who sometimes stayed for months, included Cesar Romero, Joan Crawford, *Gone With the Wind* author Margaret Mitchell, Supreme Court Chief Justice William O. Douglas, Franklin and Eleanor Roosevelt, and Lyndon Johnson. For more than thirty years, Rancho was managed by Dick Jenkins, a former stockbroker from the East coast, and his sister Nellie, a nurse. It closed during World War II, while Jenkins served in the U.S. Air Force in Asia and Europe. Other owners, who maintained it as a guest ranch, followed: In 1979, the Victoria Land & Cattle Company converted it back into a cattle operation; and in 1983, Californians Bill and Frances Davis began the massive job of restoration. Three years later, Richard Schultz bought Rancho de la Osa, and it became a Spanish-style guest ranch once again.

Today, Rancho's century-old hacienda is filled with fine antiques and international art, much of it created by artists who have visited. Though it has seen many expansions, improvements, and renovations over the years, the ranch has absorbed these changes with such grace that they appear to be totally original. One of the reasons for that is the adobe itself, whose warm hues echo the sky at sunset, and the other materials including wood and tile, that are

This page and opposite: Cactus flower hues color the hacienda and its surroundings—a melon adobe arch, a weathered blue door in a pink wall, a tangerine interior—its ceiling draped in white; and a turquoise pool under a purple sunset.

the essence of Southwestern style. Guests linger by the large fireplace in the hacienda's main room, in its cozy, colorful salons, and in the dining room with its gourmet Southwestern cuisine, fine wines, and premium tequila tastings. Territorial-style adobe guest rooms, grouped around Rancho's original courtyards, are uniquely decorated with vibrant colors and Mexican antiques; most have fireplaces. But there are no TVs or radios and few clocks. Instead, there is the mission bell summoning guests to dinner.

For guests who want to be up and out before dawn to see and hear the bird choir herald the sunrise, Rancho's staff prepares sack breakfasts. A birder's heaven, Rancho de la Osa borders the 115,000-acre Buenos Aires National Wildlife Refuge that is home to more than 300 bird species. Its grasslands protect the endangered masked bobwhite quail, and loggerhead shrikes imperiled elsewhere in the West are plentiful here. There are tanagers, cormorants, ibis, gray hawks, snow geese, falcons, osprey, cranes, phalarope, gulls, cuckoos (even the Greater Roadrunner), hummingbirds, kingfishers, ravens, larks, vermilion fly catchers, and golden eagles during their seasonal migration—the list goes on.

Weather permitting, Rancho de la Osa offers two scheduled rides a day. To encourage bonding between horse and rider, guests usually have one mount for their entire stay. That may be the only constant: The ranch aims for a varied riding experience with sightseeing rides, picnic rides, rides across varied terrain from grassland desert to rocky upland and mountain hills, loping rides (with approval by the head wrangler), and working rides rounding up horses. Rides vary in length depending on each guest's riding ability and length of stay. City slickers can borrow boots and hats from the ranch's extensive collection. On Sundays, when the horses get half a day off, there might be a "Dudeo" for guests to show off ropin' and ridin' skills.

Using Rancho's trail bikes, guests can take the slow, scenic route or try a challenging guided, ten-mile mountain bike tour through the Buenos Aires Refuge. People also connect with terra-firma hiking through the ancient rock formations on the ranch itself, in the wildlife refuge, or to Baboquivari's "rock house," where the view is a clear seventy miles into the Altar Valley of Mexico. Rancho packs bag lunches for all-day treks to Mustang Trail, the Cienega Trail, or Brown Canyon. Golfers can arrange tee times through the ranch for play on a PGA championship desert course. Within an hour's drive are a ghost town, Southwestern shopping, and several Spanish missions, including the Mission of San Xavier Del Bac, one of the nation's finest examples of this architectural style. Two must-sees are the Kitt Peak Observatory, the planet's largest center of stellar and solar research, and Saguaro National Forest and Desert Museum, which showcases Sonoran Desert plants and wildlife.

Though access is limited, the adventuresome climb Baboquivari—an ancient peak given to wild, unpredictable weather. The Tohono O'odham Indians believe the legendary figure, I'itoi, who created fire, humans, and his share of mischief, lives there. Of course, some might just buy a basket showing the mountain as a spiral with I'itoi inside and contemplate that myth as they bask by Rancho's swimming pool.

This page: A long horn above a rustic stone fireplace recalls the ranch's colorful history. Opposite: Interiors display richly textured adobe, furnished in rustic Southwestern style with antique furniture and bright Native American and Mexican textiles.

Redstone Inn

Oh, these vast, calm, measureless mountain days.... Nevermore, however weary, should one faint by the way, who gains the blessings of one mountain day; whatever his fate, long life, short life, stormy or calm, he is rich forever.
—John Muir, journal

TURN-OF-THE-CENTURY STYLE IN THE COLORADO MOUNTAINS

For more than two centuries the American frontier moved ever westward from the Eastern seaboard, until the U.S. Census officially declared in 1880 that the task of opening the frontier was finished. From the start, people were lured West to seek, make, or increase their fortunes. In the mountains of Colorado, there was more than "gold in them thar hills." Silver, copper, lead, and coal were waiting below the surface to make people rich.

Redstone, Colorado, is a town founded by coal-mining tycoons John Cleveland Osgood and J.A. Kebler. Mining companies built towns all through the mountains: Many were humble places, with wood buildings that turned ramshackle after the mine stopped producing and the money moved out. Corporate indifference, low wages, lack of sanitation, and diseases like typhoid fever plagued most coal-mining camps. Redstone was different.

Osgood came West in 1882 and bought a claim for $500 from two gold miners who were disappointed to find coal. In the next decade, he bought up all the coal claims and promising mines he could find, became sole supplier to some regional railroads, and furnished high-quality coal to metal smelters in the Rockies. He merged his company with its chief competitor to found the Colorado Fuel and Iron Company in 1892. By 1899, CF&I's beehive coking ovens in Coalbasin were smelting thousands of tons of coke that was sent twelve miles by narrow-gauge railroad to Redstone and shipped to the company's steel mills in Pueblo.

Opposite: The Redstone Inn, a picturesque Alpine-influenced Arts and Crafts building, was built in 1902 to house coal miners in Redstone, Colorado, a utopian community cofounded by tycoon John Cleveland Osgood (bottom left), who built his fortune from a $500 claim.

When Osgood began construction of Redstone in about 1900, he had already put down four strikes at CF&I by hiring strikebreakers and allowing violence—standard corporate operating procedure at the time. But Osgood wanted better things for his 16,000 workers. He hired Dr. Richard Corwin, a pioneer in the new science of sociology, to improve conditions at all CF&I operations in Colorado, Wyoming, and New Mexico. Osgood made Redstone his personal project, envisioning it as a model for his industry.

To build his utopian community, Osgood hired New York architectural firm Boal and Harnois, which used Alpine-influenced Arts and Crafts designs and unusual combinations of wood and stone, red sandstone, shingle exteriors, decorative exterior cross-framing, turrets, and hipped and gable roofs to give Redstone a unique, picturesque character.

Located on a twenty-two-acre property on the Crystal River, the Redstone Inn, designed by Theodore Davis Boal and built in 1902, was posh digs for bachelor miners—with steam heat, telephones, reading rooms, a laundry, and a barbershop. The thirty-five-room inn, now a classic old-fashioned resort, is wonderfully true to turn-of-the-century style. Rising from a base of red sandstone taken from nearby cliffs, the two-and-a-half-story wood-frame building features a square cross-timbered clock tower that extends a full story higher than its roofline. Original windows frame spectacular scenery. Interiors showcase sixty pieces of original Gustav Stickley Arts and Crafts furniture—among the many pieces shipped from New York—perhaps as Osgood's reminder to his employees of the value of superior workmanship. Ornate fireplaces, an original tapestry, rich wood paneling, period lighting, and expansive views from its verandas make a guest feel downright baronial. There's also a high level of craft in the form of great food in the inn's two popular restaurants.

The entire town of Redstone was built in a three-year period. It boasted fire hydrants, a fire station, and a clubhouse with a theater and library. There were eighty-eight chalet-style cottages with standard floor plans and singular ornamentation for foremen and miners with families. Osgood's 150-acre estate was nearby. Every

Redstone Inn
82 Redstone Boulevard
Redstone, CO 81623
800-748-2524
www.redstoneinn.com

building featured electricity from Osgood's hydroelectric plant, as well as indoor plumbing—a rarity at the time—with running water piped in from a reservoir above town. Thanks to Corwin, Redstone had a school with a kindergarten, a night school with classes in sewing, cooking, and hygiene, and a company magazine with articles about child care, education, and healthful recreation. It also had a bathhouse and a rule: Miners were to stay off the streets until they bathed and changed clothes.

Redstone is smack-dab in the middle of some of the best skiing, fishing, and other outdoor activities in the Colorado Rockies. It is surrounded by the White River National Forest and Snowmass Wilderness Area, and is about an hour's drive from Aspen's ski slopes. There are plenty of cross-country trails at McClure Pass Summit, Bogan Flats, Spring Gulch and Coal Basin, and Ute Meadows Nordic Center. The inn has a fitness center, swimming pool, and tennis court. Sleigh rides, rafting, horseback riding, golf, hiking, and biking are nearby, and there's catch-and-release fishing (with a five-rods-a-day limit) on a half mile of privately stocked river at the Redstone Preserve. The world's largest hot-spring pool is a forty-five-minute drive away in Glenwood Springs, and Redstone is on the West Elk Scenic Byway, a seven-hour driving loop for scenic and heritage travel.

Opposite: A horse-drawn carriage, an original tapestry adorning a baronial mantel, and the Redstone Inn's cross-timbered clock tower, which extends a full story above the roofline. This page: The main staircase retains its period details.

Today, the community of Redstone, population less than one hundred, is a rare, virtually intact example of a company town. Its main boulevard is a wonderful historic district replete with cottages containing shops, galleries, and cafés. Several miles away, the Coke Oven historic site displays the old industrial structures that helped make Osgood one of the richest men in America. Redstone Castle, the 24,000-square-foot, forty-two-room mansion Osgood called Cleveholm Manor, is a must-see. Designed by Boal and built in 1903, it resembles a sixteenth-century Tudor manor house. Its lower two stories are cut-and-coursed red sandstone; its upper portions are wood-shingled; and it's rich with towers, turrets, and oriel windows. In 2003, the IRS seized the castle. The inn's owners stepped in to help preserve it, and its staff arranges tours there from Memorial Day weekend through mid-October and coordinates special events.

Osgood's company's success made CF&I a takeover target, and by 1903, after two such attempts rendered it insolvent, he turned over control to Eastern investors led by John D. Rockefeller. In sympathy with striking coal miners in the East, CF&I workers staged a walkout, and CF&I slowly dropped its humanitarian efforts. But the town of Redstone, and Redstone Inn, survive from his early utopian idea.

This page and opposite: In the inn's guest rooms, rich colors, white woodwork, and original moldings and diamond-paned windows create a warm backdrop for turn-of-the-century furnishings, including sleigh beds and sixty original Gustav Stickley Arts and Crafts pieces.

Sanctuary on Camelback Mountain

To go 'up to the mountain' or 'into the desert' has
become part of the symbolical language.... Here...
the most familiar realities recede and others come
into the foreground of the mind and heart....
To have experienced it is to be prepared to see
other landscapes with new eyes.
—Joseph Wood Krutch, *The Voice of the Desert:
A Naturalist's Interpretation*, 1955

HEALTH AND WHOLENESS IN THE MOUNTAIN'S EMBRACE

From Camelback Mountain, which rises 2,700 feet
above Arizona's Paradise Valley, a figure sculpted by
wind and water in the ancient red sandstone looks
out across the desert. The natural phenomenon, an
eighty-foot-high tower on the northwest side of the
two-summit mountain, has long been known locally
as "the Praying Monk." He or she—some Buddhist
monks are women—is the visual reference point for
the holistic upscale resort, Sanctuary on Camelback
Mountain. The centerpiece of the fifty-three-acre
resort, located ten miles outside of Phoenix, is its spa,
and a single word client Scott Lyon spoke to the architects—"Zen"—was the wellspring of its appearance
and approach.

In 1999, when Lyon and Bill Nassikas of Westroc
Hospitality and architects Ken Allen, Mark Philp,
and Jon Heilman of the Scottsdale-based firm Allen +
Philp first saw the property, the beauty of the mountainside was almost obscured by a raft of tennis courts,
part of a dated and very tired resort. In the 1950s, one
of Frank Lloyd Wright's protégés, architect Hiram
Hudson Benedict, had designed a pro shop, casitas
and courts at the Paradise Valley Racquet Club. In
1965, the club was sold to local investors, who added
casitas, creating John Gardiner's Tennis Ranch. In
addition to celebrity charity tournaments, the ranch
helped create a preserve that eliminated development

Opposite: Paradise Valley's Sanctuary on Camelback Mountain
counterpoints angled and curved lines, smooth and rough textures, and
neutral and bright colors to create a sense of life in balance. Bottom:
A 1950s clubhouse got a twenty-first-century facelift.

above the 1,700-foot level of Camelback Mountain.
The place changed hands—and names—after that, but
always remained a resort.

As Allen and Philp walked the site, between the
old club's courts and casitas arranged in terraces on
the slope, they noticed points where the view looked
toward the rock formation. The Monk was the perfect focal point for Lyon's idea. But the structures did
not complement the site: They perched on the land,
rather than seeming part of it. Even desert vegetation
had been stripped away. The dual-purpose pro shop/
clubhouse was so rundown that a visiting feng shui
consultant pronounced it impossible. Before the place
could do its part to restore the stressed-out and overworked, it required extreme rejuvenation itself.

And before the architects could transform the spa
concept and Lyon's keyword into the three-dimen-
sional language of buildings, they had to fully understand the essence of what had become stylish, often
empty buzzwords of the new millennium. As they
knew from having designed other spas, the term "spa"
originated when therapeutic mineral springs in the
Belgian town of Spa became synonymous with health
resorts. The concept of the spa was older, tracing its
roots in occidental culture at least to the hot springs of
Bath, England, discovered and named *aquae solis,* or
"waters of the sun," by the Romans in the first century A.D.

The literal meaning of the word "meditation,"
the practice fundamental to Zen, is "wall gazing."
Meditation quiets the mind and produces serenity. To
the architects, this suggested a certain kind of wall,
austere and ordered. They drew upon Buddhist concepts of the five elements as a way to set the look and
feel of the space: earth, fire, metal, wood, and water.
Each has specific qualities: the earth's stability and
support, water's fluidity and sparkle, fire's warmth
and radiance, the flexibility, strength, and endur-
ance of wood, the expansive properties of metal. Each
element is also associated with a specific shape: for
instance, water with the circle, earth with the square,
fire with the triangle. Working with these concepts,
Allen and Philp set out to create a context where the
interplay of architecture, artwork, music, landscape,

Sanctuary on
Camelback Mountain
5700 East McDonald Drive
Paradise Valley, AZ 85253
800-245-2051
www.sanctuaryoncamelback.com

food, and creature comforts would lift everyday stresses from the mind, please all five senses, and engender rest, relaxation, and renewal.

Its setting, along with service and attention to guests, creates the experience people have of the Sanctuary on Camelback Mountain as a serene and calming retreat, a place to be in harmony not only with nature but with oneself. Yoga, tennis, swimming in four heated pools, hiking and biking on resort trails, access to world-class area golf courses and desert horseback riding, and rock climbing (even on the Monk, a climb not for novices) afford guests plenty of chances to push the muscles and work up a sweat. There are museums and cultural events in nearby Phoenix and Scottsdale, including Frank Lloyd Wright's studio in Scottsdale, where programs emphasize his theories of organic design. But the essence of the Sanctuary on Camelback Mountain is the return to the calm center, the chance to breathe deep and emerge restored.

With the Monk above the site and the foot of the mountain below, the strongest site-planning issues were how the buildings should transition up and down the slope, and how to incorporate both straight sight lines across the valley and meandering ones affording unexpected views of the Monk. The architects conceived of the resort's paths as a journey with multiple gateways through which the imagination could move, and with destinations, in Buddhist terms "the lotus seat," on which to rest.

The site plan and the buildings flowed from these ideas. The architects reorganized, rebuilt, and reskinned the walls of the clubhouse and peeled back its roof to open views to the mountain. They created an infinity-edge pool on the site of the centermost tennis court, resurrected the tired casitas, and designed two dozen new ones. They introduced curves to Sanctuary's twelve-by-sixteen-inch concrete-block construction, so the buildings seem to emerge organically from the earth. They reference the soft lines of adobe construction, but without its heaviness. Below and around the clubhouse, casitas hug curving paths that trace the contours of the mountainside. Strong architectural elements are

This page: Casitas are linked by flowing paths oriented toward Camelback Mountain's Praying Monk rock formation. Opposite: Elements of water and fire at the infinity edge pool; a path; an awning shades a casita patio; entry to the main building.

defined in hues bright as desert flowers, drawing the eye ever forward. As one moves along the paths, new vistas open and new destinations are seen, always with the Monk as the visual touchstone.

Sanctuary's ninety-eight mountainside and spa casitas, terraced into the mountain's north slope, are havens of tranquility. The seventy-four remodeled casitas are appointed with luxury linens and duvets, travertine marble baths, and votive-decorated tubs. Within the turreted entries of the resort's twenty-four luxury spa casitas, guests are greeted by a view of Paradise Valley. Each has a private terrace and fireplace framed in a maple-veneered wall. Opposite them, blocks made of aggregate from the nearby Salt River and tapered to smoothness form a splayed masonry wall. The palette takes its tones from the desert: One bright-hued wall is offset by an otherwise neutral scheme that incorporates honed gray terrazzo, the russet maple, the greens and grays of the jojoba plant.

Sanctuary's 12,000-square-foot indoor/outdoor mountainside spa comprises eleven treatment

This page and opposite: A casita's simple entrance offers no clues to its stunning interior. Whimsical figures guard the spa lobby's slit window, which offers a view of the Monk. Casitas are furnished in a palette of desert hues.

rooms offering Oriental and Occidental techniques, a Watsu immersion pool, a state-of-the-art fitness center, weight room and movement studio, a seventy-five-foot-long shaded outdoor lap pool, a tennis compound, steam baths, a meditation garden, and a meditation area with a reflecting pond. Packages include the five-day escape that the resort calls "Satori," the Japanese word for enlightenment. The spa's water features recall the origins of Paradise Valley's transformation into the lush area it is now, by the Hohokam Indians, who dug 135 miles of irrigation canals diverting the waters of the Gila and Salt Rivers between A.D. 700 and 1400.

Fittingly, the Sanctuary's rejuvenation included reintroduction of desert flora. That and the choice of art subtly enhance the spa experience. Indigenous plants attract birds and provide sensory pleasures: the sound of birdsong, the scent of creosote and mesquite, the taste of spa-grown herbs used in the resort's restaurant. Appropriately called 'elements,' it serves sophisticated farm-fresh cuisine in a minimalist setting that includes a community table for guests dining alone and for couples who want to break bread with new acquaintances. Both 'elements' and the Sanctuary's 'jade bar' offer sweeping views of the valley. A collection of nonrepresentational works by regional artists, all influenced by the Orient, engages

the viewer and enhances a contemplative atmosphere. "Three things are needed for beauty," wrote Thomas Aquinas, "wholeness, harmony, and radiance."

Sanctuary's East-meets-West approach underscores how spiritual concepts resonate from culture to culture. The idea, for instance, of the "circle of the spirit" is prominent in Native American beliefs as it is in Tibetan ones. Sacred sites seem to pass from one civilization to another. Archaeologists believe that the Hole-in-the-Rock in Phoenix's Papago Park was the spiritual center of Hohokam civilization. Today, Pima, Tohono O'odham, and Hopi Indians consider it a sacred place. An opening in the ceiling of a rock shelter, Hole-in-the-Rock directs the noon rays of the sun onto different points on the floor, which the Hohokam marked to develop seasonal calendars used in agricul-

ture. It is only one of many archaeological sites in the area. Another is Camelback Mountain's Ceremonial Grotto, where the Hohokam made offerings to their gods. Did they also see the rock as a human figure? If so, what did they call it? Shaman, Benedictine, or Bodhisattva, the Praying Monk isn't indicating any religious preference, except for the obvious one expressed in the peace and calm in that centered northward gaze. Sanctuary on Camelback Mountain offers a little piece of that, too.

Sun Mountain Lodge

We are part of the earth and it is part of us. The perfumed flowers are our sisters. The bear, the deer, the great eagle, these are our brothers. The rocky crests, the dew in the meadow, the body heat of the pony, and man all belong to the same family.
—Chief Seattle, letter, 1854

A PEAK EXPERIENCE IN THE WASHINGTON CASCADES

Sun Mountain Lodge sits on a 3,000-foot-high peak in the Cascade Range of north-central Washington, overlooking the tranquil, glacier-carved Methow Valley. The road from Winthrop winds through the wilderness to the mountaintop, until at last it ribbons across meadowlands to a building that seems hewn from the mountainscape. So sensitive is the area's ecology, which includes the 1.7-million-acre Okanogan National Forest, that developers planning large-scale ski resorts and condominium projects have gone elsewhere. People around here think that's just fine.

One thing that sets Sun Mountain Lodge apart in this era of industrial tourism is its adherence to the ethic that small is indeed beautiful. With ninety-six guest rooms, the lodge is alone on its mountaintop, commanding unspoiled 360-degree views of tree-covered slopes and vivid blue lakes and skies. Sun Mountain's buildings are simple, straightforward structures that complement their magnificent natural setting.

The original lodge was a fifty-room enterprise designed by well-known Seattle architect Roland Terry and built in 1968 for its first owner, Jack Barron. It comprised a main building with a dining room and lounge and two buildings containing guest rooms overlooking Gardner Mountain and Patterson Lake. Terry fit his buildings ideally to their sites and used rough materials in sophisticated ways. At Sun Mountain, he used massive timbers, huge local boulders, and fossil-embedded stones. Principally a residential architect, Terry created interiors that were both dramatic and comfortable.

In 1987, Erivan and Helga Haub, a German couple who vacationed in the Cascades, bought 3,000 acres of mountain with the facilities Terry designed—and bought into strict guidelines for development that would preserve its ecology. The task of renovation and expansion went to the Seattle office of NBBJ, a process-oriented architecture and design firm. Architect Rick Buckley and interior designer Christopher Larson took their cues from Many Glacier Lodge and Timberline, two of the buildings that defined Northwest style for generations of architects. The Haubs and NBBJ agreed that Sun Mountain had to be environmentally responsive and sized appropriately, engage the local community, and remain true to Terry's original vision and style. The buildings they inherited from Terry had proportions that were generous but not overblown, possessed a strong connection to the earth, framed the views through large expanses of glass, and incorporated a sense of craft. Like the park lodges, they were designed to collaborate with the landscape.

The Haubs also wanted the resort to reflect the history and character of the area. The northern Cascades were Native American hunting grounds for 9,000 years before trappers came here in the 1800s. In 1868, gold was discovered nearby; the Methow Valley's first orchard was established in 1888; and in 1891 a little community was founded by Guy Waring at the fork of the Chewuch and Methow Rivers. Winthrop still maintains the character of a frontier town, with a main street of terrific authentically restored false-front buildings. Waring's Duck Brand Saloon now serves as its town hall, and his home survives as one of a collection of chinked-log buildings at the Shafer Historical Museum. The area's artistic leanings date from early on. Winthrop was named after nineteenth-century author, adventurer, and traveler Theodore Winthrop; Gardner Mountain after Boston art patron Isabella Stewart Gardner; and Waring's Harvard roommate Owen Wister wrote *The Virginian* after honeymooning here. Today, Winthrop and nearby Twisp boast local

Sun Mountain Lodge
P.O. Box 1000
Winthrop, WA 98862
509-996-2211
www.sunmountainlodge.com

Opposite: Alone on a mountaintop overlooking Washington's Methow Valley, Sun Mountain Lodge was designed in the tradition of America's great national park lodges and with sensitivity to the natural environment. Winter activities include sleigh rides and tobogganing.

theater, summer music festivals featuring chamber music, rhythm and blues, and old-time fiddlers, art galleries, and a cadre of dedicated craftspeople.

NBBJ created a master plan for the forty-five acres immediately surrounding the resort. Though the Haubs owned primary water rights, the idea of a golf course was scrapped, because maintenance would consume so much of a precious resource. To provide electricity and new water and sewer systems, they partnered with local companies. The project included all new guest accommodations. The two-story motel-like Gardner building was rebuilt on its original footprint as a log structure to match the main lodge; it houses twenty-eight guest rooms with wet bars and gas fireplaces overlooking the Cascades. The new, secluded Robinson building, intended for longer stays, offers twenty-four deluxe rooms with gas fireplaces and views of Methow Valley. And a new extension to the main lodge contains an additional forty-seven guest rooms. There are also sixteen cabins at nearby Patterson Lake.

The lion's share of the work was in the main lodge, whose outstanding original feature was a dining room extending from the building's core over Methow Valley. Keeping its massive log interior, NBBJ added a cantilevered section extending it farther. Architects morphed Terry's small lounge into a grand two-story lobby like those in the national park lodges. Construction was a challenge, because all building materials and furnishings had to be brought up the mountain, and because builders wanted to minimize intrusion on the environment.

The lodge's massive timbers and details, like a split-log bar, Idaho quartzite flooring in the lobby, and a private dining room in a rock-walled, 5,000-bottle wine cellar, recall early chinked-log construction and the era when mining created overnight millionaires. Interior design emphasizes honest materials that will age gracefully over time, such as decorative antiques, comfy chairs, and carpets of wool rather than synthetics.

But it is the work of Methow Valley artisans that best expresses Sun Mountain's pride of place. The quantity and quality of handcraftsmanship that the lodge showcases is extraordinary, particularly for a

This page and opposite: The lobby's handcrafted details include a custom chandelier, a front desk featuring carvings depicting area wildlife (modeled on Timberline's) and a vintage Neoclassical key receptacle, and an intricately hewn mantel.

new building, and makes Sun Mountain one-of-a kind. The lobby's desks are carved with wilderness images similar to those created by WPA workers in the 1930s at Timberline; the mantels on the fireplaces are hand-hewn of wood; and its massive chandelier is crafted of saw blades, chains, and old farm implements. Guest rooms are enlivened with armoires and tables by area cabinetmakers, fireplace screens and andirons by local blacksmiths, and quilts designed and sewn by local women with fabrics supplied by the lodge. More than decor, this is a rich array of storied objects.

Sun Mountain boasts more than thirty-seven miles of groomed cross-country ski trails, connected to the 109-mile Methow Valley system, one of the largest groomed ski-trail systems on the continent. The lodge offers ski instruction and equipment, sleigh rides, and ice skating on site. It can arrange heli-skiing in the Cascades, and there's Alpine skiing at Loup Loup Ski Bowl a short distance away. In the summer, there's swimming, horseback riding, hay-wagon rides, kayak-ing, canoeing, rowing, sailing, hiking, tennis, moun-tain biking, golf at Bear Creek Golf Course, and fishing on nearby lakes and streams. Sun Mountaineers, a summer program for children ages four to ten, offers

nature walks, crafts, and sports. Guests visit the North Cascade Smokejumper Base to learn about parachut-ists who fight forest fires or to practice riding cavalry-style at a cavalry school. Rafters can take on Methow River's Class IV rapids or float lazily past meadows, orchards, forests, basalt cliffs, and into the lower val-ley's desertlike conditions.

The Okanogan National Forest, with elevations ranging from 2,000 to 7,000 feet, offers 1,600 miles of trails. The area is rich with wildlife, including the largest migratory mule deer herd in Washington. It was their case, argued successfully by the U.S. Forest Service before the U.S. Supreme Court, that discour-aged at least one big development in this corner of the world. When people meet up with these creatures at Sun Mountain, thank-yous are often exchanged.

This page: Dinner in the wine cellar. Opposite: The cantilevered dining room extends into the view; it and the adjacent bar emphasize natural textures and bold lines. Guest rooms showcase quilts, furniture, and art by Methow Valley craftspeople.

Sundance Resort

My earliest memory of Sundance is the sweet smell of the pines, and then the wild waterfall and the bright stream racing down the canyon.... The first week at the Institute was devoted to improving our scripts.... After each of these sessions, I would hike up to the waterfall and let the new ideas wash over me.... Walking along the singing stream gave me peace, and more often than not, I found inspiration at its source. Then the actors arrived and the Institute became a beehive of creative activity.
—Anne Makepeace, "Sundance, A Brief Personal History," essay, 2004.

SYNERGY BETWEEN ART AND NATURE IN THE MOUNTAINS OF UTAH

In 1961, when a relatively unknown twenty-five-year-old actor paid $500 for a two-acre piece of land in a remote area of Utah and built a log cabin by hand for his young family, it was just a modest getaway from New York and Los Angeles. Still a hideaway, Sundance, as it's now known, is a 6,000-acre wilderness sanctuary, an arts community with a renowned institute for independent filmmakers, and a 450-acre ski and summer resort. The Sundance Festival, a showcase for independent films, held in Park City each January, lends a glamorous cachet, but Sundance Village, in North Fork Provo Canyon, about an hour away from Park City, retains the simple, rustic aesthetic that Robert Redford always envisioned.

Located in the shadow of Mount Timpanogos in the Wasatch Mountain Range, Provo Canyon was once a summer hunting ground of the Ute Indians. Its rich folklore includes a story of how Toopanocus and his wife stayed in the area after the tribe had left, and how jealousy brought them to a bad end, with his blood coloring the caves and her tears forming Bridal Veil Falls. Early in the twentieth century, Andrew Jackson Stewart and his family established homesteads here

Opposite: At Sundance Village, in North Fork Provo Canyon, Utah, no roofline rises above the treeline. Actor Robert Redford, who founded the Sundance Institute for independent film, established the resort and its outstanding cultural programs.

and farmed. In 1947, they opened a ski resort called Timphaven, complete with a simple rope tow and a hamburger joint built around a seventy-foot pine tree. Its first lift, a single chair, was just under half a mile long. The area around Sundance was also sheepherding country, but the importation of inexpensive synthetic wool from Asia put an end to that industry and left the area open for large-scale development, which would have threatened the area's ecology. To prevent that, Redford bought 5,000 acres of land from the Stewarts in 1968, the year before *Butch Cassidy and the Sundance Kid*—his second major film role—was released. As an actor, Robert Redford is known for his restraint, and that quality pervades the resort at Sundance Village.

Though financial advisors initially advocated maximizing return on his investment, Redford opted to focus more on preservation than development. That emphasis on sustainability rather than profit has characterized Sundance ever since. Commerce—the resort, a cable-TV channel, a general store and catalog business—subsidizes culture and ecology, as Redford continues to seek the right balance between art and business, preservation and development, community and individuality.

The same issues play out in the nonprofit Sundance Institute Redford founded in 1981. A pioneering initiative, the Institute supports producers, directors, playwrights, screenwriters, actors, and composers whose work in the highly collaborative worlds of film and theater reflects a compelling, original vision. Sundance's intensive laboratories offer emerging artists the freedom to experiment under the guidance of veteran filmmakers and theater professionals. Programs include the development of Native American cinema artists. The Institute's laboratories have been the source of a steady stream of creative products, many of which have earned top awards, and all of which have contributed unique and original voices to the country's cultural heritage. The Sundance Institute has arguably done more in its history to nurture artists working in film, and to exhibit new, independent documentary and dramatic films,

Sundance Resort
RR3, Box A-1
Sundance, UT 84604
800-892-1600
www.sundanceresort.com

than any organization in the United States.

The most visible of the Institute's programs is the annual Sundance Film Festival, a ten-day event that attracts an international audience. Showcasing the best American and international independent films, the festival offers a lively menu of screenings, concerts, and other activities in Park City, Salt Lake City, Ogden, and at the resort in Sundance Village.

Sundance didn't add accommodations until 1988, seven years after the establishment of the film Institute. Blending into the wooded contours of the fifty-acre village are post-and-beam buildings that include a spa and restaurants, townhouse rental condominiums and cottages, and privately owned houses. Their placement affords privacy, and their architecture and varied decoration emphasize natural materials and native colors.

Sundance's environmental sensitivity and its spirit of creativity are evident everywhere. The resort's spa incorporates wood trestle lumber salvaged from the Great Salt Lake, water-saving devices, energy-efficient lighting and heating, and wallboard made from sunflower seed hulls. Cottage deck chairs are made of 100-percent-recycled milk jugs. The resort's restaurants use tableware that includes pieces crafted from recycled wine bottles in an on-site glassblowing studio, an imaginative and practical way to recycle glass bottles and jars.

The fare in Sundance's seven eateries, based on fresh and organically grown ingredients, many from its own farms, is equally creative. Timphaven's restaurant around the pine tree became Sundance's gourmet Tree Room, where the decoration includes a wall-size nineteenth-century Ute rug, part of Redford's collection of Native American art. The Foundry Grill offers breakfast, lunch, and dinner. There are two cafés for skiers, a deli, a private club for members called the Owl Bar, and gourmet fare at Zoom in Park City.

Sundance's art program is one of the best to be found anywhere. Its Art Shack is a busy place, offering workshops taught by resident and guest artists. Guests may be up to their wrists in clay forming a wheel-thrown bowl, perfecting the curve of a bracelet, concentrating on their charcoal or pencil drawings, or heading off down the trail with watercolors or photographic equipment. There are painting, photography, and sculpture exhibits, lectures

This page and opposite: From the interior of its earth-friendly spa, to its rehearsal hall, to Provo River fly-fishing, to après-ski sunning at Bearclaw—the interplay of art and nature makes Sundance a singular place.

by noted authors, a summer outdoor film festival on site, summer concerts by the Utah Symphony in the resort's outdoor amphitheater, and performances by singers and songwriters in the Bluebird Café series imported from Nashville to Sundance's Owl Bar. In the evenings, people might gather for Native American storytelling and drumming or a lecture on ecology. At Sundance, creativity breeds new ideas and programs every year.

In the summer, there's horseback riding through mountain meadows and groves of aspen, riding instruction, hiking, mountain biking, and a day camp for kids. Rocky Mountain Outfitters is on hand to furnish equipment for virtually any outdoor adventure a guest could want. As for fly-fishing, some sections of the Provo River are estimated to contain up to 3,400 trout per square mile, with the average rainbow or brown trout measuring around seventeen inches. There's even spelunking in three linked caves with spectacular formations and colorations at Timpanogos Cave National Monument.

At Sundance, unspoiled terrain, Utah powder, and a 2,150-foot vertical drop mean great boarding and skiing. Downhill skiers will find forty-one runs for all skill levels, and no crowd; the largest lift is a quad. There's cross-country skiing on fifteen miles of trails; ski and snowboard instruction; a ski school; all-day supervision for kids; snowshoeing on six miles of trails; and day and moonlight cross-country ski and snowshoe tours guided by naturalists and ornithologists. Balloon and glider rides, dogsledding, snowmobile tours, sleigh rides, and ice skating are within driving distance.

Utah's mountain and canyon ecosystems are fragile, and there's a dedicated local effort to preserve them. Redford and his family are active in the North Fork Preservation Alliance, which protects open spaces and wildlife and promotes sustainable development. In 1998, they donated 860 acres as a conservation easement to Utah Open Lands. "This is my gift to my community, myself, and most of all, my children," Redford said, "to pass on to their children, so they can experience the land as something real rather than as something seen in movies, described in history books or only imagined."

This page: Redford describes Sundance as "...a mixture of old and new, lush and spare, sophisticated and primitive—like art itself." Opposite: A studio on site recycles wine bottles into glassware for Sundance's Tree Room and Foundry Grill restaurants.

Tanque Verde Guest Ranch

There were cow ponies in a corral, and one of them would not be caught, no matter who threw the rope.... The man might pretend to look at the weather, which was fine; or he might affect earnest conversation with a bystander; it was bootless. The pony saw through it.
—Owen Wister, *The Virginian* (1903)

SECLUSION AND TRAIL RIDING IN THE SONORAN DESERT

The dude ranch is an extraordinary phenomenon that could only have developed in America. No one is exactly sure who was responsible for the idea, but in about 1880, a few Western families began to entertain friends from the East who paid for room and board so they could stay as long as they liked. The idea caught on. Much of the credit for the popularity of the dude ranch goes to books (and later, films) that glamorized the life of the cowboy, and, in particular, author Owen Wister. Born in Pennsylvania and educated at Harvard, Wister spent several summers in Wyoming for his health and fell in love with the Western frontier. His stories and books, particularly his famous novel, *The Virginian*, published in 1903, fascinated armchair travelers in the East. Before long, tenderfeet were flocking to ranches in the West—actually paying money to work as cowboys so they could experience firsthand the kind of life that Wister had so effectively described.

Located 2,800 feet up in the lush foothills of the Rincon Mountains east of Tucson, the Tanque Verde Guest Ranch is one of the most luxurious of country inns, but the lifestyle here vividly reflects the fact that, for well over a hundred years, Tanque Verde has been one of the most successful ranch operations in Arizona. Today, it is both a working ranch, with some 700 head of cattle grazing over 65,000 acres, and a guest ranch.

The ranch's name means "green pool" in Spanish, a reference to this area east of Tucson that rises out of the valley. Rich in the desert's most treasured natural resource—water—the location was an ideal settlement, originally for the ancient Hohokam Indians, later for the nomadic Pima Indians, and still later for cattlemen who established their ranches here.

Tanque Verde, one of the oldest ranches in America used as a guest facility, was founded in 1868 by Rafael Carillo, who was born in Santa Cruz, Sonora, Mexico, in 1842, some twenty years after the Mexican Revolution ended Spanish rule in the desert Southwest. In 1856, three years after the Gadsden Purchase established the U.S./Mexico border in its present location, Carillo moved his family to Tucson. By 1860 he was farming some forty miles east, where Apache raids were frequent and violent. In 1868, he returned to Tucson and founded the ranch, which he named the Buena Vista. As it prospered, he renamed it La Cebadilla, after the wild barley growing near Tanque Verde Creek.

Carillo officially registered the ranch's 'R/C' brand in 1904. After his death in 1908, the ranch passed to Jim Converse, who worked it as a cattle ranch. Converse heard about a successful dude ranch being run by the Eaton brothers in Wolf, Wyoming, and in the 1920s followed their lead, transforming his working cattle ranch into a dude ranch and renaming it Tanque Verde. Converse was an expert rancher and hunter and a terrific storyteller, whose wild Western manner entranced guests from the East. But in 1945, after accidentally shooting a man, he lost interest in ranching. Brownie Cote, who owned the Desert Willow guest ranch in Tucson, purchased Tanque Verde in 1957; his family continues its traditions today.

The centerpiece of Tanque Verde is horseback riding, with about 150 mounts and ten full-time wranglers. In the morning, guests can ride to breakfast at the ranch's old stone homestead, then take to the trails again for the second ride of the day. The trail ride may wind around the countryside, across meandering streams, up into the Rincon Mountains, or through the Sonoran Desert. In the winter, there's a rodeo for kids where they can try barrel racing, pole bending, and keyhole reining.

Tanque Verde Guest Ranch
14301 East Speedway
Tucson, AZ 85748
800-234-3833
www.tvgr.com

Opposite: Near Tucson, the pink adobe exterior of guest rooms at Tanque Verde Ranch, one of the oldest ranches in America used as a guest facility. Wranglers relax on the *ramada*, or porch, and junior wranglers earn their spurs.

Horseback riding is by no means the only activity at Tanque Verde. The ranch's roster of day and evening activities includes tennis, swimming and lounging by the indoor or outdoor pools, guided hiking and mountain biking, fishing, volleyball, basketball, yoga, art classes, country-swing and line dancing, and programs focusing on astronomy, desert flora and fauna, and cowboy and Native American lore. There's golf at one of the championship courses nearby, and shopping in Tucson or Nogales, Mexico. Tanque Verde also has meeting facilities, and its Desert Awareness Center is wired for voice and data connectivity, including a high speed T1 data line. Of course, some guests prefer to just snooze in a hammock while waiting for the next barbecue.

Bordered by the 63,000-acre Saguaro National Park to the south and the rugged 1.385 million-acre Colorado National Forest to the east, the ranch claims desert wildlife as its nearest neighbors. Guests can explore nature on guided daily walks through the Sonoran Desert. The Tanque Verde is a bird-watcher's paradise, and birds seem to be everywhere, singing the guests to sleep at night and waking them in the morning.

Tanque Verde's main building, built in 1863, is a solid, L-shaped ranch house with walls almost two

This page and opposite: A wooded path, a barbecue, a guest suite, a decorative wagon wheel, a shady log-fenced corral, and an outdoor patio at sunset provide opportunities for seclusion and socializing, depending upon a guest's mood.

feet thick, a spacious, graceful place that has the feeling of an elegant inn. Its card room comes with its own legend. A long time ago, bandits broke in, demanding that Carillo disclose the location of the $85,000 he was supposed to have stashed away. When he refused, they strung him up from the nearest beam. Fortunately, Carillo lived, but the story recalls a time when being on a ranch wasn't the vacation it is now.

Today, guests requiring a little pampering after a day in the saddle will find indoor and outdoor whirlpools, as well as massages and other treatments at the ranch's La Sonora Spa. Accommodations are in stylish and comfortable Western-appointed rooms. Most of the ranch's seventy-four rooms have their own adobe fireplaces, and each leads out to a private lounging area. All have modem jacks and phones.

One of Tanque Verde's most popular spots after a day on the trails is the Dog House Saloon, where guests gather around a huge stone fireplace, billiard table, and hand-carved mesquite bar. Barbecues, scheduled twice a week, include live music; on other nights, the ranch's dining room offers delicious food that satisfies. Afterward, it's tempting to simply relax with a glass of wine and debate whether today's gold, coral, and purple sunset surpasses yesterday's.

This page: After a trail ride through Sonoran Desert terrain rich with Saguaro cacti and plant and animal life, including many bird species, guests might lounge poolside soaking up the Arizona sun.

Teton Ridge Ranch

I wanted to be the first to view a country on which the eyes of a white man had never gazed and to follow the course of rivers that run through a new land.
—Jedediah Strong Smith

CIVILITY AND STYLE IN THE GRAND TETONS
Comprising a scant seven guest suites on 4,000 acres surrounded by protected wilderness, Teton Ridge Ranch, just forty miles from Jackson Hole, feels just as far away from the resort's bustling ski enterprises as a person can get. Located in Tetonia, Idaho, on the west side of the Grand Tetons, the ranch offers the serenity of a mountain retreat along with every computer-age amenity one could wish for, with access to the action at Jackson less than an hour's drive away.

Built in 1985 in the tradition of a mountain lodge, the ranch's commodious 10,000-square-foot main building combines the sheltering heft of lodgepole pine construction with soaring expanses of glass that frame a spectacular view. In the living room, log walls and massive beams rise from polished wideplank flooring to a cathedral ceiling, and stone fireplaces and porches, identical to those in the dining room, afford intimate places to gather. Because the ranch accommodates such a limited number of guests, intimacy is a byword. Teton Ridge's dining room, for instance, with its huge window and view and its adjoining library, is the perfect setting for a candlelit gourmet dinner by the fire. Five spacious suites in the main lodge and two more in a private guest cottage a short amble away are havens—individually decorated with Western-style furnishings, down comforters, and original artwork, and equipped with wood-burning stoves.

Surrounded by the Targhee National Forest, adjacent to the Jedediah Smith Wilderness Area, and near Grand Teton National Park, the ranch is a place for virtually every outdoor activity imaginable—even shooting sporting clays. Teton Ridge has a stocked

Opposite: The entrance to Teton Ridge Ranch, in Tetonia, Idaho, an hour's drive from Jackson Hole, is marked by a timbered crossbar, in traditional Ranch style. The main lodge and guest cottages are havens in all seasons.

pond and is close to some world-famous fly-fishing at Henry's Ford and the Teton and Snake Rivers; its fishing guides know which waters are best in each season. For adventurous rafting, the Snake River churns up plenty of white water, and the park's waters offer lazier scenic float trips. Guests hike or mountain bike on the ranch's twenty miles of trails, or take a summer chairlift ride at Grand Targhee and walk down the slopes for a grand view of the Tetons.

That same chairlift is a stairway to heaven for downhill skiers. Cross-country skiers explore the ranch's groomed trails and innumerable backcountry trails in the adjacent forests and wilderness area. Teton Ridge has no structured dude ranch program, but once the heavy snows are gone, guests can ride every day if they want. In winter, people ice skate, join the head wrangler on the sleigh that delivers hay to the horses, or go out with a dogsled team that departs from the front door of the lodge. Some venture farther for a snowmobile tour of Yellowstone or to ride behind dog teams that train in Jackson Hole for Alaska's famed Iditarod race. Teton Ridge's staff tries to make each stay an individual experience, so guests feel like they are visiting a private home with exceptionally accommodating hosts.

The ranch's site, atop a 6,800-foot knoll, assures an unspoiled view of mountains and meadows favored by wildlife, and of a valley that was hunting ground for the Absaroka Crow, Gros Ventre, Blackfeet, and Shoshone Indians who followed game across the Great Divide, a meeting point for fur trappers, and the route the Nez Perce Indians took in their desperate 1877 attempt to reach Canada.

The Tetons are rugged country, among the youngest mountain ranges in the West. Two separate uplifts occurred to create them, the first about fifty million years ago, the second, beginning nine million years ago. Cycles of cooling and warming over the last two million years caused glaciers to advance and retreat; they sculpted Jackson Hole and other valleys and deposited till to create moraines. Behind these, water collected, forming lakes.

The most perilous part of Meriwether Lewis and

Teton Ridge Ranch
200 Valley View Road
Tetonia, ID 83452
208-456-2650
www.tetonridge.com

William Clark's 1804–06 expedition was crossing the Bitterroot Range from the east into what is now Idaho; they lost horses and precious supplies, winter was coming, and there were few animals to hunt. As they emerged from the mountains, they encountered Nez Perce Indians, who supplied fresh provisions. That expedition opened the way for trappers, who braved treacherous conditions for the ready money they made satisfying gentlemen's demand for beaverskin top hats. In 1816, a trapper named the Tetons, from a French word meaning "breasts." In 1829, fur trader William Sublette named one of the valleys that trappers called a "hole" for his partner, David Jackson. Their third partner was Jedediah Strong Smith, who had read accounts of Lewis and Clark's expedition as a boy, and is credited with exploring more unknown territory than any other mountain man. Smith was the first explorer to travel overland to California through the Southwest, a journey that took him from the central Rockies, to Arizona, and across the Mojave Desert.

Mountain man Jim Bridger, the first white man to happen upon the Great Salt Lake in 1824, was one of a group that bought out Smith and his partners in 1830 and led an army survey through Jackson's Hole in 1840. In conjunction with his explorations of Yellowstone, geologist Ferdinand Hayden made several trips to the Tetons, naming Jenny, Leigh, Bradley, and Taggart Lakes and Mount Moran after members of his 1872 survey. Jenny was the Shoshone wife of mountain man Beaver Dick Leigh, one of Hayden's guides; she and their children all perished of smallpox. The expedition's photographer, William H. Jackson, created some of the finest images ever made of the Tetons. Once Yellowstone was designated a national park later that year, tourists came, along with settlers, who in 1884 built the area's first homesteads north of Jackson. Early in the twentieth century, guides began escorting wealthy game hunters into the Tetons, and the area got its first dude ranch.

All this development, which occurred throughout the West, devastated Native Americans, who lost their ancestral lands to the white men, saw their children shipped off to schools that replaced their rich cultural

This page and opposite: In the main lodge, massive lodgepole pine timbers frame windows with spectacular views. Wide plank floors, timbered walls and ceilings, and stone fireplaces give the living and dining rooms a distinctly Western flavor.

legacy with a new and strange one, died of foreign diseases like smallpox, and were removed, one way or another, to make way for settlement and commerce. The Nez Perce lost part of their Oregon reservation when gold was discovered there. In 1877, some young braves fought back and the entire tribe fled, battling the U.S. Army in a 1,500-mile pursuit that took them through the Tetons, toward Canada. Hungry and exhausted, they were forty miles from the border when the Army attacked. The survivors were split up among reservations in Oklahoma, Idaho, and Washington. Nez Perce Chief Joseph's 1877 speech is among the most poignant in American history. "I am tired of fighting," he said. "Our chiefs are killed…. The old men are all killed…. It is cold and we have no blankets. The little children are freezing to death. My people, some of them, have run away to the hills and have no blankets, no food; no one knows where they are, perhaps freezing to death…. Hear me, my chiefs, I am tired; my heart is sick and sad. From where the sun now stands, I will fight no more forever."

In a happier time, the Nez Perce chief said something else. "The earth and I are of one mind." That's a feeling that comes naturally here, even if one's idea of enjoying the great outdoors is to read a book on a porch overlooking a mountain meadow. Yet it took generations to shape Grand Teton National Park and preserve the wilderness areas around it. In 1897, the Teton Forest Reserve was set aside by Congress. In 1908, President Theodore Roosevelt established Targhee Forest, named in honor of a Bannock Indian warrior; the Shoshone-Bannock tribe has ancestral treaty rights to use it. In 1929, Congress set aside the Teton Range and six glacial lakes at the base of the mountains, an area a third the size of the current park, as Grand Teton National Park. When local residents fought expansion of the park, John D. Rockefeller Jr., one of the nation's wealthiest men, quietly began buying land in the area in order to preserve it. In 1943, by presidential proclamation, President Franklin Delano Roosevelt combined Teton National Forest, other federal properties including Jackson Lake, and land donated by Rockefeller to create Jackson Hole National Monument. Finally, in 1950, the government

reached an agreement with Teton county and local landowners; Congress combined the existing park and the monument to create Grand Teton National Park. Rockefeller's son Laurence, active in environmental causes throughout his life, deeded additional acreage. The U.S. Congress designated Wyoming's Jedediah Smith Wilderness in 1984.

This system of parks, forests, and wilderness areas surrounding Teton Ridge Ranch is part of the twelve-million acres of the Greater Yellowstone Ecosystem, the largest area of relatively undisturbed plant and animal habitat in the contiguous United States. It's a land of deer, elk, moose, bighorn sheep, bald eagles, and grizzlies—one of the nation's rare wild places, and one of its last.

This page: Decorative details, such as antique wooden shoe forms on a country dresser, a landscape painting, Native American-inspired textiles, and lanterns on a timbered staircase, create warm and interesting interiors. Opposite: Enjoying the grandeur of the Tetons in winter.

Timberline Lodge

A good many of us probably think of our forests as having the primary function of saving our timber resources, but they do far more than that...(they) provide forage for livestock and game, they husband our water at the source; they mitigate our floods and prevent the erosion of our soil. Last but not least, our national forests provide constantly increasing opportunity for recreational use.
—Franklin D. Roosevelt, 1937

A RARE WORK OF ART FOR SNOW LOVERS
When President Franklin D. Roosevelt dedicated the impressive ski lodge at Timberline, 6,000 feet up on the southern slope of Mount Hood, he called it "a monument to the skill and faithful performance of workers." Timberline is the result of a unique public-works project, the largest in American history. Its construction began in 1935, in the depths of the Great Depression, at a time when one in four American wage earners was out of work. Hundreds of men and women were hired by the U.S. Works Progress Administration and the Civilian Conservation Corps to clear the land and build and furnish the 74,000-square-foot Lodge. Timberline was the first WPA project of its kind: a government-owned recreational facility built on National Forest Service land and financed principally with public funds. It was, said WPA administrator Emerson Griffith, "distinctly an experiment, to get away from the leaf-raking type of project.... It was to be a monument to the skill, and industry of the unemployed, and it is a monument the world will have to acknowledge."

The Forest Service intended Timberline, located in Mount Hood National Forest, to emphasize scenic preservation, demonstrate the talents of local artists and craftsmen working with local materials, and exemplify the pioneer spirit of the West. Though Timberline does that and more, its design

Opposite: Built by the WPA and Civilian Conservation Corps workers during America's Great Depression and opened in 1937, Timberline, on Mount Hood, sixty miles from Portland, Oregon, defined a new style of architecture called "Cascadian."

came after several missteps. Faced with ideas that included a nine-story glass skyscraper, which many, including prominent landscape architect Frederick Law Olmsted, thought horrifying in that setting, the National Park Service turned to Harvard-trained architect Gilbert Stanley Underwood, whose accomplishments included lodges at the Grand Canyon, Yosemite, and Zion and Bryce Canyon National Parks.

Underwood drew a plan in the "National Park Rustic" style for a rugged building similar to other wilderness lodges. However, Forest Service architects Tim Turner, Linn Forrest, Dean Wright, and Howard Gifford had other ideas, and they are credited with the lodge's design. The team came up with an alternate plan for an expansive but elegant stone, clapboard, shingle, and board and batten building that resembled the country estates in and around Portland, just sixty miles away. What the two plans had in common was their roots in the era's Arts and Crafts design movement, which emphasized the quality of handwork and the use of natural materials in natural settings. The style that emerged is called "Cascadian," after the mountain range where Mount Hood stands. If there were ever an exception to the dictum that nothing good is ever designed by committee, Timberline is it.

Underwood's plan gave the lodge a style to match the mountains; Gifford, Wright, Turner, and Forrest gave it refinement. Underwood envisioned two wings of unequal length connected by a central core he called the "head house," something "brutal in scale, as it should be, to merge properly with its surrounds." He wrote, "... The interior columns... will be high and massive.... entirely of peeled log construction, held together with hand-wrought iron bands...very bold in character." The Forest Service architects reoriented the building on its site, placing its back to the wind and to inevitable winter snowdrifts. They retained the wing and core design, anchored each wing with a massive stone chimney, and developed a roofline that seems to follow the contour of the mountain. An intricate geometry of hipped and shed-roofed dormers,

Timberline Lodge
Timberline, OR 97028
800-547-1406
www.timberlinelodge.com

"short-term project" to design Timberline's interior, an assignment that lasted four years. Smith's designs repeated lines and forms taken from the architecture. In the lobby, for instance, curved three-cushion sofas and six-sided tables and lampshades echo the shape of the room. This repetition, she wrote, produces a pleasing "rhythm and pattern the single design does not possess."

To showcase the crafts of wood carving, black-smithing, cabinetmaking, and weaving, designs were created and produced specifically for Timberline. More than one hundred skilled artisans worked in Portland's public school buildings creating the hand-crafted decorative objects. By the 1930s, blacksmiths were a vanishing breed, but under the direction of a master smith, the men learned the skill and cre-ated a unique collection of hand-wrought iron gates, chandeliers and light fixtures, andirons, escutcheons, hinges, door knockers, window grilles, and other ornaments, some in animal forms, like the coyotes on the iron gates leading to the Cascade Dining Room. Prototypes of the hefty wooden furniture were built on site, and if successful, were blueprinted for repro-duction. The simple but massive furniture is con-structed of wood with strap irons; chair and bench seats were made of laced rawhide; chair backs and tabletops are crafted from thick hardwood planks. Oregon women fashioned spun-copper ashtrays, made 119 hooked rugs, wove 912 yards of drapery and furniture textiles, appliquéd fabric, and sewed one hundred pairs of curtains. The nonprofit Friends of Timberline replicates and replaces worn-out textiles with reproductions based on the originals and contin-ues the lodge's tradition of supporting and teaching craftspeople.

The interiors of Timberline's public rooms are a study in contrasts, combining light and dark, inti-macy and grandeur. In the lobby—a room the size of a small cathedral—the ninety-two-foot-high hexagonal chimney soars through the ceiling, and forty-foot timbers of peeled pine support the roof structure. Yet fine details and a rugged stone fireplace bring what could have been an almost intimidatingly

some arranged in tiers, cascade down the slope of the roof, which nearly meets the ground. They modified Underwood's lobby from an octagon to a hexagon and rotated it to the south. They kept the peeled-log con-struction but dropped some of Underwood's ideas of brutality and lack of ornamentation, in favor of rustic yet sophisticated custom details.

Three hundred sixty feet long, four stories high, and topped by a 750-pound bronze weathervane, Timberline cost about $1 million to build. It couldn't be duplicated today for fifty times that much. Italian stonemasons, who had completed the Columbia River Highway, taught unskilled Americans their craft. Together, they took some 400 tons of volcanic stones from nearby canyons, chiseled them into shape, and lifted them into place to make the central chimney structure. The forty-foot pine pillars that support the roof of the central space were cut in the Gifford Pinchot National Forest in Washington, then hand-hewn by broadax and smoothed by adz. Woods used in the interiors include Western juniper and hem-lock, Port Orford cedar, and Oregon white oak, and the woodwork includes relief carvings of woodland scenes, motifs taken from a Campfire Girls hand-book, and an arch that Turner and Forrest designed.

Portland designer Margery Hoffman Smith, active in the Arts and Crafts movement, was hired on a

Opposite: Timberline's unique interior displays stunning craftsmanship: a hexagonal lobby with a 92-foot chimney and balcony, hand-carved wood and stone, custom metalwork, and art, including a glass mosaic of Paul Bunyan in the bar. This page: The shingled roofline and pool.

large space down to manageable proportions. On the wooden staircases, newel posts are made from cedar utility poles, each carved on top in the shape of a native bird or animal. They now wear the patina of the hands that have touched them appreciatively as guests ascend and descend those stairs. A balustrade of sawed-off poles borders the Ram's Head Bar and forms a balcony around the lobby. The front entry is an 1,800-pound door, hand-hewn of ponderosa pine and with iron fittings so impressive they would make a Norseman blink. The lodge's balcony offers sweeping views of Mount Hood's forested slopes, the valley far below, and Mount Jefferson forty miles to the south.

The highest peak in Oregon at 11,235 feet, shimmering with eleven glaciers and first scaled in 1857, Mount Hood is the most popular snowcapped mountain climb in North America. Timberline offers a ten-month season of snowshoeing, snowboarding, and skiing, which has been considered among the world's finest ever since a group of sportsmen from Portland first broke trails in 1906. On a busy weekend, thousands pass through its ski facilities in contemporary Wy'East Day Lodge. Yet in this setting, guests have the feeling of being tucked away in natural wilderness. There's swimming year-round and, in summer, plenty of forest and meadow trails to roam.

Timberline's Cascade Dining Room lets diners savor the grandeur of the building and the view, along with gourmet cuisine that focuses on Northwest ingredients, including fresh-caught salmon. Its seventy guest rooms range from generously proportioned ones to others of modest size. Some have rock fireplaces and touches of luxury and elegance, including corner desks of blond wood.

Art, all by artists employed by the WPA, is everywhere here, and includes Howard Sewall's panels showing Timberline's builders; Thomas Laman's mosaic *Spring on the Mountain;* Virginia Darcé's glass mosaic depicting Paul Bunyan and Babe in the lodge's Blue Ox Bar; Douglas Lynch's incised linoleum murals; and oil paintings by Charles Heaney, Darrel Austin, and C.S. Price. Even hallways and guest rooms still feature works by WPA artists, including lithographs and botanical watercolors Smith found in a cardboard box in Portland.

Perhaps the most telling details about Timberline are not the architectural or decorative ones but the human ones. When Civilian Conservation Corps workers finished construction, they gave their worn-out uniforms and blankets to be used as material for the more than one hundred hooked rugs Oregon women made to decorate the rooms. At a time when being employed mattered so much, some of the lodge's builders stayed on the job for only two weeks, to give others the chance to earn a living. What makes Timberline a great building is that its design, craftsmanship, and social history express something about the greatness of the human spirit. It's this quality that has inspired the heartfelt dedication to maintain its character through time, and that continues to impress even a casual visitor.

This page and opposite: Timberline's astonishing decorative details include rugs based on originals crafted by Oregon women from the shirts off construction workers' backs, newel posts carved in the form of eagles, a ram's head table base, and virtuoso ironwork.

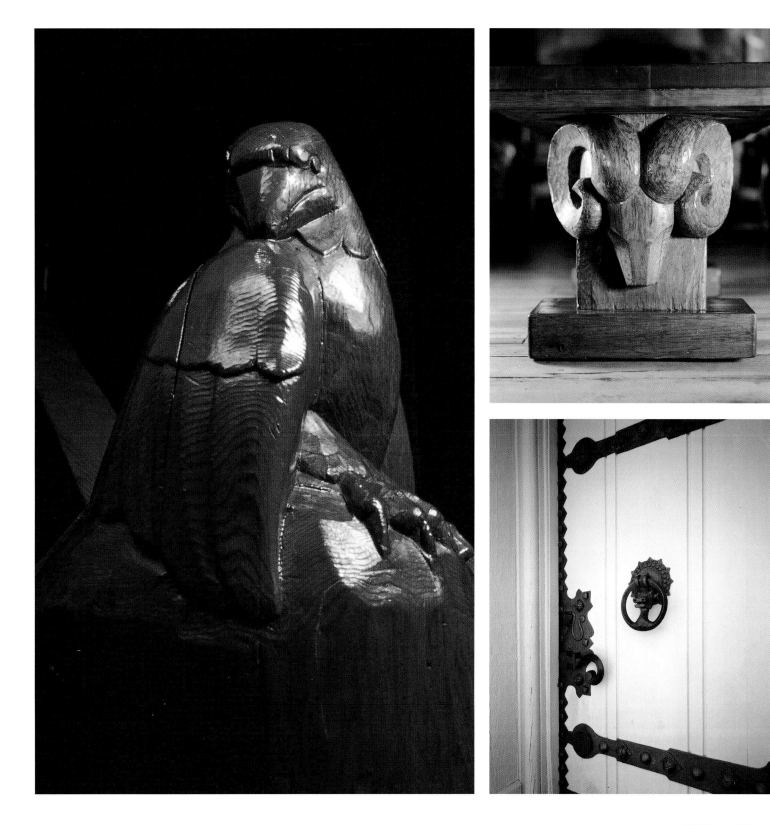

Vista Verde Guest Ranch

Water—the ace of elements. Water dives from the clouds without parachute, wings or safety net. Water runs over the steepest precipice and blinks not a lash. Water is buried and rises again; water walks on fire and fire gets the blisters. Stylishly composed in any situation—solid, gas or liquid—speaking in penetrating dialects understood by all things—animal, vegetable or mineral—water travels intrepidly through four dimensions, sustaining... destroying... creating..."
—Tom Robbins, from the preface to *Even Cowgirls Get the Blues*

ELEGANCE AND EMERALD PASTURES ON THE CONTINENTAL DIVIDE

The Elk River flows from a hidden wilderness on the Continental Divide, high in the Rockies of north-central Colorado. Over millennia, the river has etched narrow canyons, watered wide glacier-made meadows, slaked thirsty forests of evergreen and aspen. Elk, deer, and bear drink its waters; trout leap sparkling from the bright churn of its current. In the high Elk River Valley, surrounded by national forest lands and ribbon forests of lodgepole pine, a secluded guest ranch takes its name from the verdant mountain views.

Only about twenty-five miles north of Steamboat Springs, Vista Verde Ranch is a high-valley sanctuary, an escape into a quiet, natural world, a ranch that delivers all the comfort of a resort. For unknown centuries, the perennial springs and mountain licks along the ridge above the ranch have attracted game. The Ute, one of the Indian tribes indigenous to Colorado, camped and hunted by the springs. Trappers and mountain men crisscrossed this part of the Rockies on the Wyoming Trail; mining settlements were formed nearby in the late nineteenth century; and Clark, the nearest town, was settled in the 1890s. In 1908, by presidential proclamation, Theodore Roosevelt created the Medicine Bow-Routt National Forest, which borders

Opposite: On the Great Divide, adjacent to Medicine Bow-Routt National Forest and near Steamboat Springs, Colorado, the log buildings of Vista Verde Ranch, a high valley sanctuary, are tucked between a mountain meadow and a protective ridge, where perennial springs attract deer and other game.

the ranch. The circumstances, recorded in Roosevelt's autobiography, are an object lesson in political maneuvering:

"While the Agricultural Appropriation Bill was passing through the Senate, in 1907, Senator Fulton, of Oregon, secured an amendment providing that the President could not set aside any additional National Forests in the six Northwestern States. This meant retaining some sixteen million acres to be exploited by land grabbers and by the representatives of the great special interests, at the expense of the public interest.

"But for four years the Forest Service had been gathering field notes as to what forests ought to be set aside in these States, and so was prepared to act. It was equally undesirable to veto the whole agricultural bill, and to sign it with this amendment effective. [So, I approved] a plan to create the necessary National Forest in these States before the Agricultural Bill could be passed and signed.... I signed the last proclamation a couple of days before, by my signature, the bill became law; and when the friends of the special interests in the Senate got their amendment through and woke up, they discovered that sixteen million acres of timberland had been saved for the people by putting them in the National Forests....

"The opponents of the Forest Service turned handsprings in their wrath; and dire were their threats against the Executive; but the threats could not be carried out, and were really only a tribute to the efficiency of our action."

When the Medicine Bow-Routt National Forest was created, neighboring lands were divided into homesteads. Eight years later, the Blair family claimed this remote homestead; and in 1919, they received title to 160 acres. The Homestead Act of 1862 required settlers to build a cabin and a barn. The ranch's old barn, constructed of spruce logs put together with mortise-and-tenon joints, recalls that chapter of its history. The ranch's next owner, Hollis Tufly, added the barn's hayloft and pitched roof, stock pens, and a chicken coop. He dug irrigation ditches, developed hay production, managed a hunting and fishing camp, and added other

Vista Verde Guest Ranch
P.O. Box 465
Steamboat Springs, CO 80477
800-526-7433
www.vistaverde.com

homesteads to create the present-day ranch. The 1936 honeymoon cabin Tufly hand-built is a secluded destination for cross-country skiers and, in summer, trail riders stop to breakfast there.

Since 1975, Vista Verde, now some 540 acres, has both been a working ranch and a guest ranch. It is rich with timothy, bluegrass, clover, brome, and other natural grasses, a reminder that this is the part of Colorado where working ranches still thrive. About one hundred cows and calves graze Vista Verde's pastures in the summer, and it is a year-round home to a remuda of seventy-five horses. The upper wetlands of the two creeks that flow through the ranch are home to many rare species and qualify for protection under a Nature Conservancy easement.

Vista Verde's stylish lodgepole buildings, pro-

tected by a ridge to the north, accommodate about forty guests in the main lodge and in nine spacious private cabins along a small stream, each furnished with a wood stove, lodgepole pine beds, antiques, and a porch with an open-air hot tub. There's a bar and billiard table at Sweetheart's Parlor, a favorite gathering place, a fitness center with workout equipment, a Nordic center outfitted with all sorts of seasonal outdoor equipment from boots and skis to bikes and fly rods, and an outdoor deck where kids can splash in fountains of water. Even the barn—the core of any ranch—turns function into elegance. While waiting for their mounts, guests enjoy the view from the rocking chairs on its porch, or watch horses being saddled from a gallery. Thoughtful landscaping includes details like walkways edged with subtle lighting that respects the show the stars put on at night.

The mountains put on a show, too. The best way to experience it is to swing up into the saddle, tackle some fly fishing, try dogsledding, or strap on a pair of skis or snowshoes. Vista Verde is small enough to

This page: Outdoor activities include fly-fishing, skiing and riding, even in winter, when horses are up to their girths in pristine powder. Opposite: Paths meander to guest cabins with porches and views and bridge a stream near the barn.

cater to each person's interests. Its team of guides scouts the best terrain and conditions on the ranch property and in neighboring wilderness areas, and can lead the way in fly-fishing, horseback riding, rock climbing, rafting, hiking, biking, skiing, and snowshoeing. There are activities designed for kids and teens, so families can stay together or head off in different directions. If an activity—like skeet shooting or lap swimming—isn't offered at Vista Verde, it's likely to be nearby.

Skiers, both beginner and expert, take advantage of the 300 to 400 inches of fluffy powder that falls in the Elk River Valley every winter on nineteen miles of groomed trails, and there's backcountry Nordic skiing across frozen lakes, open meadows, through pine groves, and on nearby mountains.

Horseback rides are limited to groups of three to five people, so each ride can be tailored to skill level and interest. The ranch matches horses and guests based on riding experience and personality. All-day adventures include picnics on Wapiti Mountain with its views of the Continental Divide, in the depths of Hole-in-the-Wall Canyon, or at the wildflower-studded Farwell Meadows. But Vista Verde is about more than scenic trail rides. There are lessons and clinics for greenhorns and advanced riders, and riders can work sorting steers. That's a handy skill to have in the ranch's weekly team penning and trail ride competitions, or for its June and September cattle drives. These are adults-only, but otherwise everyone can ride daily. People who'd rather sit behind a horse than on one can learn how to drive a team of draft horses like the ones that pull the ranch sleigh in winter, delivering hay to the horses. Winter riding at Vista Verde, on a horse wearing its thick winter coat, breathing steam into the air, and up to its girth in pristine powder may be one of the most exquisite riding experiences in the world.

In fact, it's hard to decide whether the winter or the summer is better here. One thing's certain: When a ten-year-old wanna-be angler snags his first trout and the ranch's chef gives it gourmet treatment and serves it up for dinner, it can make a kid forget all about that computer game in his suitcase.

This page: In winter, a sleigh delivers hay to the horses. Opposite: Cowboys and cowgirls of all ages find adventure at Vista Verde, which tailors activities to guests' interests. Comfortable Western style includes riding tackle adorning a guest cabin.

The Willows Historic Palm Springs Inn

The [desert's] rainbow hills, the tender bluish mists, the luminous radiance... trick the sense of time... You always mean to go away without quite realizing you have not done it.... For one thing there is the cleanest air to be breathed anywhere.... Someday the world will understand that, and the little oases... will harbor for healing its ailing, house-weary broods.
—Mary Austin, *Land of Little Rain*, 1903

COMFORTABLE GLAMOUR AT A 1920s VILLA IN PALM SPRINGS

The desert of Palm Springs, located on eighty-three-square miles of land about 110 miles southeast of Los Angeles, has been a healing oasis since the days when the band of Cahuilla Indians that Spanish settlers called "Agua caliente," after the "hot water" of the springs, camped here among the bunches of palms.

During the nineteenth century, Victorians recognized the healthful qualities of the dry desert air, just as they discovered "physical culture" and the value of exercise; in the late 1800s, the Southern Pacific Railroad began running trains through the open desert. The first American automobiles were manufactured in 1895, and as they became more affordable (the price of a basic Model T Ford dropped from around $800 in 1908 to about $270, or about one-half the average family's annual income, by 1924), newly mobile tourists flocked to America's western deserts to enjoy the dry climate, get fresh air and exercise, and heal a variety of ills. From then on, Palm Springs and its neighboring communities—among them Desert Hot Springs and Rancho Mirage—grew into playgrounds for the famous and fabulous.

In 1927, New York lawyer, self-made multimillionaire—and asthmatic—Samuel Untermyer bought a home—now the Willows Inn—on the rocky lower slope of San Jacinto Mountain. Reportedly the first attorney in America to command a million-dollar

Opposite: The Willows, Palm Springs, built in the Italian Mediterranean style with three-foot-thick concrete walls, was the vacation home of New Yorker Samuel Untermyer, reportedly the first attorney in America to command a million-dollar fee.

fee for a single case, Untermyer, born in 1858, was a Virginian of German descent. His father, a Jewish tobacco planter, lost his fortune in Confederate bonds and died, history relates, of shock and grief after General Lee's defeat in the Civil War. In 1867, Untermyer's widowed mother moved to Manhattan, where she supported her family by operating a boardinghouse. Untermyer, whom William Jennings Bryan would call "America's greatest lawyer," graduated from Columbia University at age twenty, earned national prominence in law, and served the New York City and federal governments. Perhaps most famously, he led a Congressional investigation into J.P. Morgan's Money Trust and abuses on the New York Stock Exchange and argued an anti-Semitism case against auto magnate Henry Ford. At his Yonkers, New York, estate, Untermyer indulged his passion for gardening, and in particular, the raising of orchids. Known for the dramatic structure of his arguments—which included making Morgan wait for hours while he examined lesser witnesses—Untermyer wore his orchids as boutonnieres in the courtroom.

From the start, residences in Palm Springs and other desert communities indulged an appreciation of exotic lands and other playgrounds and borrowed building ideas from those places. Untermyer's villa was built in Italian Mediterranean style, with three-foot-thick concrete walls reinforced with steel, a vaulted ceiling with vast mahogany beams resting on carved sandstone Corinthian capitals in the Great Hall, a living room with a hand-carved sandstone fireplace, and a dining room that features a rose-stone floor, a fanciful painted coffered ceiling, and a fireplace with antique ceramic tiles imported from Spain. On his four acres in Palm Springs, Untermyer developed gardens and orchards; landscaping at the Willows Inn still includes fruit trees, native flora, and the bougainvillea he planted beside the fifty-foot waterfall that cascades down a cliff behind the mansion.

It was the perfect setting to entertain the luminaries of the era, including Clark Gable and Carole Lombard, New York mayor Jimmy Walker, and Albert Einstein and his wife, Elsa, who visited often and

The Willows Historic
Palm Springs Inn
412 West Tahquitz Canyon Way
Palm Springs, CA 92262
800-966-9597
www.thewillowspalmsprings.com

stayed long. A decade after Untermyer died in 1940, actress Marion Davies, mistress of publishing giant William Randolph Hearst and owner of the Desert Inn, took up residence. The eight guest rooms at the Willows Inn today, appointed with antiques dating from its heyday, include the Einsteins' room and Davies' suite.

If this suggests the villa has always been the pinnacle of chic, it has not. In 1993, when its current owners, physicians Tracy Conrad and Paul Marut, emerged from dinner across the street at the gourmet restaurant Le Vallauris, and first saw it, just next to the Desert Museum in Old Palm Springs Village, Untermyer's villa was a train wreck of taste—a Budweiser sign hanging from the dining room's frescoed ceiling, black wallpaper with fuchsia-pink moldings in the Davies bedroom, and red carpeting, smoked mirrors, and dropped ceilings throughout.

Though it was not their plan to buy, renovate, and operate an inn, Conrad and Marut found themselves hooked by the place with "beautiful bones" that looked so neglected. It was the Einstein story, as much as the house itself, that decided it. Other former visitors to the mansion—titans of industry, famous politicians, Hollywood movie stars—paled next to the mustached

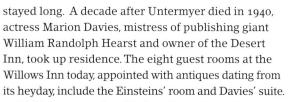

This page: The inn is set on the lower slopes of San Jacinto Mountain. Opposite: Rooms and gardens flow together to create an airy retreat, marked by Mediterranean touches, such as a mosaic vaulted ceiling and an intricate ironwork gate.

genius who trod the footpath to the villa's "Inspiration Point" to watch the sunrise and ponder the mysteries of the universe.

Conrad and Marut restored the public spaces and guest rooms to their original grandeur, fixed fireplaces, equipped each of the eight bedrooms with a luxurious bath and furnished them with antiques such as a burled Italian bedroom set and a blond bird's-eye maple sleigh bed, revived Untermyer's gardens and waterfall, repaired the heated swimming pool, installed a Jacuzzi, and added such twenty-first-century amenities as computer ports. Their restoration took more than two years, meticulous attention to detail, and every spare penny they had. Today, the inn's guests can take a tram ride up the mountain, play golf or tennis, hike or horseback ride nearby, or have a night out at one of Palm Springs' many clubs, the Indian-run casino, or the Plaza Theater's Palm Springs Follies. Then, they can luxuriate between fine linens on an antique bed, relish gourmet breakfasts overlooking the waterfall, lounge on one of the inn's private patios, or meditate, as Einstein once did, on Inspiration Point. Now, as then, the villa's comfortable glamour is as warming as the desert sun.

This page: A palm-shaded gate leads to the garden. Opposite: The Willows' tradition of entertaining encompasses dinners alfresco. Untermyer's friend Albert Einstein was a frequent visitor, whose room and favorite outdoor spot, Inspiration Point, remain intact.

Acknowledgments

First and foremost, I am grateful to David Larkin, whose erudition, generosity, and sense of fun are only three of the qualities that make him one of the best book guys in the world. I'm beholden to Elric Endersby, of the New Jersey Barn Company, for introducing us.

At Rizzoli, editor Jane Newman has shown unflagging grace, responsiveness, and intelligence, all much appreciated. Thanks to Adam Michaels for his design and composure under pressure.

Lily Jones, my favorite and only daughter, deserves kudos for her patience while I was working on this project. It's a gift to have a child who inspires you to be your best, and Lily does.

Finally, my thanks to the owners, managers, public relations and advertising people, Web masters, architects, photographers, curators, photo librarians, and others associated with the destinations included in this book, and especially to those who were my contacts: David Abe, Linny Adamson, Allan Affeldt, Ken Allen, Susan Anaya, Michael Anderson, Noelle Aune, Debra Austin, Jan Betts, Bruce Black, Randi Jain Black, Jessica Boyd, Bruce Brossman, Rick Buckley, Brian Charlton, Tracy Conrad, Sally Cooper, Kathie Curley, Clare Evans, Christy Eugenis, Marie Fortin, Mike Gildersleeve, Lisa Govan, Elizabeth Gullickson, Anjali Holchand, Kerri Holden, Scott Horne, Kelli Huth, Judy Jordan, Kathleen Kaul, Nina Kumana, Christopher Larson, Tania Lee, Erica Lennard, Scott McGehee, Tom and Mona Mesereau, John Munn, Lisa Ness, Joe Pellegrini, Joan Phillips, Mark Philp, Sally Pierce, Jenny Powers, Mike Quinn, Tanya Raedisch, Simone Rathle, Lucy Ridolphi, Richard Saler, Janet Sample, Veronica Schultz, Josie and Doug Smith, Susan Spaeth, Cas Still, Debbie Strom, Rob Thorlakson, Kimberly Tucker, Debbi and George Van Etten, Alex Vertikoff, Jess Vogelfane, Bobbie Wade, Rick Wargo, Amy Wessell, and Palmyre Zele.

GLADYS MONTGOMERY

Reprint Permissions

Page 14: By Annie Dillard, from *Pilgrim at Tinker Creek,* copyright © 1974. Reprinted by permission of HarperCollins Publishers Inc.

Page 26: By Larry M. Dilsaver and William Wyckoff, from *The Geographical Review,* 1997. Reprinted by permission.

Page 56: By Joseph Wood Krutch, from *The Voice of the Desert,* copyright © 1954, 1955 by Joseph Wood Krutch. Renewed 1992 by Marcella Krutch. Reprinted by permission of HarperCollins Publishers Inc.

Page 68: By Gene Autry, from "Gene Autry's Cowboy Code," copyright © Autry Qualified Interest Trust. Reprinted by permission.

Page 80: By Cole Porter, © 1944 (Renewed) WB Music Corp. (ASCAP). All rights reserved. Reprinted by permission of Warner Bros. Publications U.S. Inc., Miami, FL 33014.

Page 104: By Paul Bowles, from *The Worlds of Tangier,* copyright © 1958 by Paul Bowles. Reprinted by permission of the Wylie Agency Inc.

Page 116: By Jackson Browne and Glenn Fry, copyright © 1978 by Swallow Turn Music. Copyright renewed. All rights reserved. Reprinted by permission of Warner Bros. Publications U.S. Inc., Miami, FL 33014.

Page 134: By Mabel Dodge Luhan, from *Winter in Taos,* published by the Las Palomas de Taos Foundation. Reprinted by permission.

Page 140: By Octavio Paz, translated by Eliot Weinberger, from *Collected Poems 1957–1987,* copyright © 1986 by Octavio Paz and Eliot Weinberger. Reprinted by permission of New Directions Publishing Corp.

Page 152: By anonymous author, from *Architectural Record,* May 1948, copyright © May 1948, *Architectural Record,* a McGraw-Hill Cos. publication. Reprinted by permission.

Page 158: By Luther Standing Bear, from *Land of the Spotted Eagle,* 1933. Reprinted by permission.

Page 164: By John Muir, from *John of the Mountains: The Unpublished Journals of John Muir.* Reprinted by permission of the University of Wisconsin Press.

Page 170: By Joseph Wood Krutch, from *The Voice of the Desert,* copyright © 1954, 1955 by Joseph Wood Krutch. Renewed 1992 by Marcella Krutch. Reprinted by permission of HarperCollins Publishers Inc.

Page 182: By Anne Makepeace, from "Sundance: A Brief Personal History," in *Sundance: The Written Word, A Series of Commissioned Essays,* 2004. Reprinted by permission.

Page 206: By Tom Robbins, from *Even Cowgirls Get the Blues.* Reprinted by permission of Bantam/Random House Inc.

Photo Permissions

Pages 2–3: courtesy of Wyndham Hotels

Pages 9–13: all courtesy of Delaware North Companies, Inc.

Pages 15–19: all courtesy of Amanresorts

Page 21: top: Sue Anaya; bottom: Ken Howie

Page 22: top: Uzair Ahmed Quraishi; bottom left and right: courtesy of Cosanti Foundation

Page 23: top: Junzo Okada; bottom: courtesy of Cosanti Foundation

Page 24: courtesy of Cosanti Foundation

Page 25: top: courtesy of Cosanti Foundation; bottom: Ayano Atsumi

Page 27: top: courtesy of Belton Chalet; bottom left and right: Jennifer Steven

Page 28: Andrew Geiger

Page 29: top: Andrew Geiger; bottom: Jennifer Steven

Pages 30–31: all Andrew Geiger

Pages 33–37: all courtesy of Wyndham Hotels

Page 39: top and bottom left: courtesy of Xanterra Parks & Resorts; bottom right: courtesy of Grand Canyon Museum Collection

Page 40: left and middle and bottom right: courtesy of Xanterra Parks & Resorts; top right: courtesy of Grand Canyon Museum Collection

Page 41: courtesy of Xanterra Parks & Resorts

Pages 42–43: all courtesy of Xanterra Parks & Resorts

Page 45: all courtesy of Cibolo Creek Ranch

Page 46: top and middle left and right: courtesy of Cibolo Creek Ranch; bottom left: Homer H. Lansberry, 1936, courtesy of Historic American Buildings Survey, U.S. Library of Congress

Page 47: courtesy of Cibolo Creek Ranch

Pages 48–49: courtesy of Cibolo Creek Ranch

Pages 51–55: all Jack Richmond, courtesy of Dunton Hot Springs

Page 57: top and bottom left: courtesy of Xanterra Parks & Resorts; bottom right: courtesy of Grand

Canyon Museum Collection

Pages 58–59: all courtesy of Xanterra Parks & Resorts

Pages 60–61: all courtesy of Xanterra Parks & Resorts

Pages 63–67: all courtesy of Canadian Rocky Mountains Resorts

Pages 69–73: all courtesy of Averill's Ranch/Flathead Lake Lodge

Pages 75–79: all courtesy of The Hermosa Inn

Pages 81–85: all courtesy of High Wild & Lonesome, LLC

Page 87: top and bottom left: Kathie Curley, Navajo Tourism; bottom right: Denver Public Library, Western History Collection

Page 88: left: Kathie Curley, Navajo Tourism; right: Denver Public Library, Western History Collection

Page 89: top: Kathie Curley, Navajo Tourism; bottom: Denver Public Library, Western History Collection

Page 90: Kathie Curley, Navajo Tourism

Page 91: left: Denver Public Library, Western History Collection; right: Kathie Curley, Navajo Tourism

Pages 93–97: all courtesy of The Inn of the Five Graces (Page 93, 94, 95 at top, and 96: Rose McNulty; Page 95 at bottom and 97: Scott Zimmerman)

Pages 99–103: all courtesy of Bruce Black

Pages 105–9: all Erica Lennard

Pages 111–15: all courtesy of Lajitas, The Ultimate Hideout

Page 117: top: Alex Vertikoff; bottom left, middle, and right: Grand Canyon Museum Collection

Pages 118–19: left and top right: Alex Vertikoff; bottom right: Mark Boisclair

Pages 120–21: left and bottom right: Mark Boisclair; top right: Alex Vertikoff

Page 123: top: courtesy of La Quinta Resort; bottom: Mike Wilson

Pages 124–25: left: Tracy Breshears; top and bottom right: Mike Wilson

Pages 126–27: top left and right and bottom left: Mike Wilson; bottom right: Arthur Cole

Pages 129–33: all courtesy of The Lodge & Spa at Cordillera

Page 135: top: courtesy of Mabel Dodge Luhan House; bottom left: Paul Gallagher, courtesy of Mabel Dodge Luhan House; bottom middle: Taos Historical Museum; bottom right: Virginia Lierz, courtesy of Mabel Dodge Luhan House

Pages 136–37: all Paul Gallagher, courtesy of Mabel Dodge Luhan House

Page 138: Paul Gallagher, courtesy of Mabel Dodge Luhan House

Page 139: all Michael Freeman

Pages 141–45: all courtesy of Amanresorts

Page 147–51: all courtesy of The Murray Hotel

Page 153: David Glomb, courtesy of the Orbit In

Page 154: left: courtesy of Joseph Pellegrini; right: Don Frank, courtesy of the Orbit In

Page 155: top left and right and bottom left: David Glomb,

courtesy of the Orbit In; bottom right: Rebekah Johnson, courtesy of the Orbit In

Page 156: left: Don Frank, courtesy of the Orbit In; right: Arthur Coleman, courtesy of the Orbit In

Page 157: top: Don Frank, courtesy of the Orbit In; bottom: Rebekah Johnson, courtesy of the Orbit In

Page 159: all courtesy of Rancho de la Osa

Page 160: Timmerman

Page 161: top left: Ellen Clark; bottom left: courtesy of Rancho de la Osa; right: Timmerman

Pages 162–63: all Timmerman

Page 165: top: John McEvoy; bottom left and right: courtesy of Redstone Inn

Page 166: top left: Stephen Deliyanis; bottom left: John McEvoy; right: David Marlow

Page 167: David Marlow

Pages 168–69: all David Marlow

Page 171: top: courtesy of Sanctuary on Camelback Mountain; bottom: courtesy of Allen + Philp Architects

Page 172: courtesy of Allen + Philp Architects

Page 173: top and bottom left: courtesy of Sanctuary on Camelback Mountain; bottom middle and right: courtesy of Allen + Philp Architects

Pages 174–75: all courtesy of Allen + Philp Architects

Page 177: all courtesy of Sun Mountain Lodge (left: Don Portman)

Pages 178–79: left and top right: Steve Hall, courtesy of NBBJ Seattle; bottom right: Paul Warchol, courtesy of NBBJ Seattle

Page 180: Ron Stark, courtesy of NBBJ Seattle

Page 181: top left: courtesy of Sun Mountain Lodge; top and bottom right: Steve Hall, courtesy of NBBJ Seattle; bottom left: Ron Stark, courtesy of NBBJ Seattle

Page 183: left: Susan Spaeth; top and bottom right: courtesy of Sundance

Page 184: top: Susan Spaeth; bottom left and right: courtesy of Sundance

Page 185: Susan Spaeth

Page 186: Scott Zimmerman

Page 187: left and bottom right: Susan Spaeth; top right: courtesy of Sundance

Pages 189–93: all courtesy of Tanque Verde Ranch

Page 195: all David Swift

Pages 196–97: all courtesy of Teton Ridge Ranch

Pages 198–99: all David Swift

Page 201: top: courtesy of Friends of Timberline; bottom: Fisher

Pages 202–3: all courtesy of Friends of Timberline

Page 204: courtesy of Friends of Timberline

Page 205: left: courtesy of Friends of Timberline; top and bottom right: Marvin Rand, Historic American Buildings Survey, 1994, U.S. Library of Congress

Pages 207–11: all courtesy of Vista Verde Ranch

Pages 213–17: all courtesy of The Willows Palm Springs

Index

The Ahwahnee, 8
Yosemite National Park
California
559-252-4848
www.yosemitepark.com

Amangani, 14
1535 North East Butte Road
Jackson, WY 83001
877-734-7333
www.amanresorts.com

Arcosanti, 20
HC 74, Box 4136
Mayer, AZ 86333
928-632-7135
www.arcosanti.org

Belton Chalet, 26
P.O. Box 206
West Glacier, MT 59936
888-BELTON5
www.beltonchalet.com

The Boulders &
Golden Door Spa, 32
34631 North
Tom Darlington Drive
P.O. Box 2090
Carefree, AZ 85377
800-553-1717
www.wyndham.com

Bright Angel Lodge &
Phantom Ranch, 38
Grand Canyon National Park,
South Rim
Xanterra Parks & Resorts
Grand Canyon, AZ 86023
888-297-2757
www.grandcanyonlodges.com

Cibolo Creek Ranch, 44
HCR 67, Box 44
Marfa, TX 79843
866-496-9460
www.cibolocreekranch.com

Dunton Hot Springs, 50
P.O. Box 818
Dolores, CO 81323
970-882-4800
www.duntonhotsprings.com

El Tovar, 56
Grand Canyon National Park,
South Rim
Xanterra Parks & Resorts
Grand Canyon, AZ 86023
888-297-2757
www.grandcanyonlodges.com

Emerald Lake Lodge, 62
P.O. Box 10
Field, British Columbia, Canada
V0A 1G0
800-663-6336
www.emeraldlakelodge.com

Flathead Lake Lodge, 68
P.O. Box 248
Bigfork, MT 59911
406-837-4391
www.flatheadlakelodge.com

The Hermosa Inn, 74
5532 North Palo Cristi Road
Scottsdale, AZ 85253
800-241-1210
www.hermosainn.com

High Wild & Lonesome, 80
P.O. Box 116
Big Piney, WY 83113
877-276-3485
www.hwl.net

Hogan Under the Stars, 86
P.O. Box 1287
Ganado, AZ 86505
928-755-3273

The Inn of the Five Graces, 92
150 E. DeVargas Street
Santa Fe, NM 87501
505-992-0957
www.fivegraces.com

Kokopelli's Cave B&B, 98
3204 Crestridge Drive
Farmington, NM 87401
505-326-2461
www.bbonline.com/nm/kokopelli

Korakia Pensione, 104
207 South Patencio Road
Palm Springs, CA 92262
760-864-6411
www.korakia.com

Lajitas, the Ultimate Hideout, 110
HC 70, Box 400
Lajitas, TX 79852
432-424-5000
www.lajitas.com

La Posada Hotel, 116
303 E. Second Street (Route 66)
Winslow, AZ 86047
928-289-4366
www.laposada.org

La Quinta Resort & Club, 122
49-499 Eisenhower Drive
La Quinta, CA 92253
800-598-3828
www.laquintaresort.com

The Lodge & Spa at Cordillera, 128
2206 Cordillera Way
Edwards, CO 81632
800-877-3529
www.cordillera-vail.com